THE REASON WE PLAY

THE REASON WE PLAY

American Sports Figures and What Inspires Them

Marc Bona

ROWMAN & LITTLEFIELD
Lanham • Boulder • New York • London

Published by Rowman & Littlefield
An imprint of The Rowman & Littlefield Publishing Group, Inc.
4501 Forbes Boulevard, Suite 200, Lanham, Maryland 20706
www.rowman.com

6 Tinworth Street, London SE11 5AL

Illustrations by Brian Shellito

British Library Cataloguing in Publication Information Available

Library of Congress Cataloging-in-Publication Data Available

Names: Bona, Marc, author.
Title: The reason we play : American sports figures and what inspires them / Marc Bona.
Description: Lanham : Rowman & Littlefield, [2021] | Includes bibliographical references and index.
   | Audience: Grades 7–9 | Summary: "More than just a collection of biographical portraits of
   famous athletes, this book also inspires middle school and high school students through the
   athletes' stories of their favorite books, what motivates them, and what obstacles they have
   overcome"—Provided by publisher.
Identifiers: LCCN 2021011751 (print) | LCCN 2021011752 (ebook) | ISBN 9781538140932 (cloth) |
   ISBN 9781538140949 (epub)
Subjects: LCSH: Professional athletes—United States—Biography—Juvenile literature. | Profession-
   al athletes—United States—Conduct of life—Juvenile literature. | Motivation (Psychology)—
   Juvenile literature.
Classification: LCC GV697.A1 B568 2021 (print) | LCC GV697.A1 (ebook) | DDC 796.04/40922
   [B]—dc23
LC record available at https://lccn.loc.gov/2021011751
LC ebook record available at https://lccn.loc.gov/2021011752

CONTENTS

ACKNOWLEDGMENTS

The idea for this book came to me years ago, but I suspect it has always been rumbling around in my brain since I was a kid. This was the type of book I enjoyed when I was young.

When I embarked on these journeys—of finding the subjects, reaching out, and researching their lives—I learned this would not be entirely a solitary project. Any book project is dependent on support from so many people, and I realized early on that was especially true for this book.

The research in finding athletes, coaches, and others formed a literary iceberg. I spent quite a bit of time on my own trying to find notable individuals who would be interested in telling me about books they read that stuck with them and advice they might have for kids. For a variety of reasons, many prospective subjects chose not to participate. My research was a constant reminder about the importance of perseverance. But along the way I had people who helped, and for that, I am grateful.

My sister, Maria Bonavoglia, brought her intelligent non-sports-fan eye to these pages to make sure my writing chapter after chapter was clear. My editor wife, Lynne Sherwin, reads everything I write, catching big-picture issues and minute problems, pointing out questions that should be asked, suggesting clarifications, and noting typos.

My neighbor, Mark Holaday, was of great assistance in connecting me with Gerry Faust. My friend Chris Lamb helped me reach out to Mike Veeck. His son, David Lamb—a sharp sports fan—took an early read and offered me a kid's perspective when he was a youngster (he's now studying sport management in college). My former colleague, sportswriter

Amy Rosewater, gladly offered advice as did prolific columnist, author, and coworker Terry Pluto. Two colleagues lent their support: Chris Quinn, vice president of content for Advance Ohio, and Chris Fedor, a beat writer for the Cleveland Cavaliers. The staff at the northwest branch of the Akron Public Library was always of service. My agent, Anne Devlin, believed in this project from the beginning. Christen Karniski, my editor at Rowman & Littlefield, guided me with a steady hand.

Brian Shellito's illustrations grace the pages. Through his eye the reader gains a clear picture of the athletes, coaches, and others, helping shape the literary portraits I tried to create.

Every one of the subjects in this book deserves a shoutout, if not a dedication. I can't thank them enough for taking time from busy schedules to answer my letters, which I wrote and mailed over several years. I had known something about everyone in here, but it wasn't until I dived into reading stories and books for my research that I came to learn so much more about them. College basketball coach Kim Mulkey was the first to respond, and receiving her letter gave me an initial boost of confidence. Tim Green, who I had interviewed for a feature story once, went above and beyond for me. He is as accomplished as an author as he was a football player. He is a testament to not wasting time, and I appreciate his willingness to contribute, as well as his gritty determination in life. Two of the subjects have since died—Todd Christensen and Frank Deford. I always enjoyed watching Christensen play and hearing him interviewed, and I loved reading Deford. Rest in peace.

Finally, if you are a youngster reading this book and want to be a writer, I encourage you to keep reading! Books open worlds and help you learn. They are an escape, and they make you think. So . . . read on!

I

BRIAN BOITANO, FIGURE SKATING

A California Kid Learns to Skate

When you think of ice skating, cold places come to mind, like Canada to the north. Or maybe Minnesota in the Midwest. But California?

Brian Boitano was raised in Northern California, in what is known as the Bay Area. When he was eight years old, his mother took him to the Sunnyvale Ice Palace to see the *Ice Follies*, a show in which skaters in elaborate costumes leap, spin, and dance. Brian was amazed. One of the skaters was dressed as a beautiful Egyptian queen. He sat in awe of the performers in their colorful costumes gracefully sailing across the ice.

After the show, he couldn't stop thinking about the performers. He had played Little League baseball, and his dad was the coach. But Brian wanted to try figure skating, and he quickly fell in love with the sport. The decision he made to give up baseball and concentrate on skating altered his life.

Brian was born October 22, 1963, in Mountain View, California, where he "had a great childhood. I was very independent and had a great imagination."[1] He also was adventurous and loved to roller skate as fast as he could and then leap and spin in the air.

So his parents started taking him to ice skate. A woman named Linda Leaver watched Brian carefully at the rink. Linda knew a lot about skating; she was a coach who had helped many young skaters. After seeing him she went home that night and told her husband that Brian was "the

best little skater" she had ever seen and one day would be a world champion.[2]

He was a quick learner and began practicing to be a top skater. "I never had to push Brian," said his coach. "He had a love of skating, of getting better, jumping higher, spinning faster, turning more times, pushing his talent to the limit. He had that drive from the very first day."[3]

In skating, jumps have different names, such as the Axel, Lutz, and Salchow. They are all named after famous skaters from many years ago. Each jump requires the skater to push off from a certain part of the skate. The word "double" or "triple" means how many times skaters can turn their bodies around in midair and land without falling. Each jump takes about one second! Years ago, competitive figure skating demanded certain shapes, or figures, be outlined on the ice. Over time, judges allowed more freestyle skating, which gave skaters more artistic freedom.

In 1982, when he was 18, Brian competed in the US Figure Skating Championships and became the first US skater to perform a triple Axel at the competition. Then a year later at the World Figure Skating Championships, he performed *six* triple jumps. And although he didn't win, he was well on his way to becoming a world-class skater.

In fact, Brian loved jumps on the ice so much there is even one named after him: the "Tano," in which he performs a triple Lutz with one hand over his head.

To become good at any sport requires a lot of hard work. Great skaters make jumps look easy, but it takes many hours of practice. "People think that skating is a sport where no one sweats or gets fatigued," Brian told a reporter once. "To make it look easy means you have to add bricks to your back."[4] With all the jumping, twisting, and landing, skaters can get hurt, and Brian had his share of injuries. While he was warming up before the 1986 US Figure Skating Championships he felt a shooting pain in his right ankle. He had reinjured a tendon, the part of the body that attaches muscle to bone. But he wasn't about to come this far and quit, so he blocked out the pain as best he could, and he won the competition.

In addition to a lot of practice, an athlete must be competitive. Brian always wanted to win, and in the course of his career, he saw many of the same skaters he competed against in different events. One of them, Brian Orser, who is Canadian, became not only his rival but also his friend. The two had been skating against each other since 1978, and the media began to call their competition "The Battle of the Brians." Many times, Orser came out ahead of Boitano.

In 1988, Brian competed on one of the world's biggest stages for sports, the Olympics. That year, the Winter Games were held in Calgary, Alberta, which is one of the 10 provinces in Canada. Alberta is in the western part of the state, and Edmonton is its capital. Skaters have two main programs, short and long, to perform in competition. They are just what their names imply: One is shorter than three minutes; the other lasts about four and a half minutes. The long program especially requires skaters to be in good physical shape. Brian went out and skated the best he possibly could. He made eight triple jumps, which had never been done before.

He was competing against Orser in Canada, Orser's home country. The crowd was divided, alternating between chants of "Boitano!" and "Orser!" But when the competition ended, Brian Boitano won the gold medal in men's figure skating. He was the only US man at those games to win a gold—the only other gold medal won by the United States that Olympics was by a woman, Bonnie Blair in speed skating. It would be 22 years before another American man, Evan Lysacek, would win a gold in men's figure skating.

What Brian made look easy took a lot of work. He put in six hours a day for six days each week for 16 years to become a great skater before he competed in Calgary. But Olympians are amateurs, and Brian had to earn a living, so he decided to join a traveling show, not unlike the one he saw when he was a boy. By doing this, he became a professional, so he no longer could compete in amateur events.

When the 1992 Winter Olympics rolled around in Albertville, France, Brian was there, but as a spectator. He had the itch to skate competitively again and felt he was in good enough shape. But he had turned professional, so what could he do? He decided to petition the International Skating Union to allow him to compete again. It took a long time, but his dream finally came true. And in 1994, Brian made the US Olympic team and traveled to Lillehammer, Norway, for the Winter Olympics. (Norway is a European country that sits near the Arctic Circle. The sea is its western border, Sweden sits to its east, and Oslo is its capital.) The change became known as the "Boitano Rule."

But all athletes eventually age, and Brian knew his time as a competitive skater was ending. So he went back to the ice shows, performing for crowds all over the country with *Champions on Ice*. He wore costumes and skated fast and jumped high for his fans. In fact, in 1988, Brian starred in *Canvas of Ice* on primetime television.[5]

Then in 2001, Brian announced the end of his career. As much as he loved skating, he was getting older and there were other things he wanted to do with his life. His parents Lew and Donna came out to watch their son perform one final time. Fellow skaters gave him gifts. Michelle Kwan, a great skater herself, presented him with a crystal vase.

Being a skater was just part of Brian's life. Media outlets like *USA Today* and ABC have counted on his expertise. He has worked with sick children through the Starlight Foundation, and he has enjoyed rollerblading around Golden Gate Park in San Francisco, a city with many steep hills near where he grew up.

In 2014, he starred in HGTV's *The Brian Boitano Project*, where he worked on fixing up an old home in Italy. But one of his biggest passions is cooking and in 2009, he got his own show on the Food Network called *What Would Brian Boitano Make*?

Through his career Brian knew other skaters looked up to him, and he had to set a positive example.

"The best role model," he once said, is "someone who's good to people."[6]

Brian says:

- Brian's favorite book: Shel Silverstein's *The Giving Tree*.
- Brian's words of wisdom: "Do something because you love to do it. Not because of what you expect to get out of it."

Shel Silverstein (1930–1999) was a cartoonist, author, and songwriter who was born in Chicago. The Giving Tree, *which came out in 1964, is about the relationship between a boy and a tree that gives him things— apples, for instance—and is happy to do so.*

2

BOBBY BOWDEN, FOOTBALL

Born to Coach

Bobby Bowden started preparing to be a coach long before he ever played organized football. Growing up in Birmingham, Alabama, Bobby and his family lived near the field where the Woodlawn High School Colonels practiced. He lived so close that he and his dad would climb atop their garage roof and watch players repeat their running, passing, and blocking drills. When he wasn't watching practice, Bobby was cutting out pictures and stories from the newspaper about his favorite team, the Crimson Tide from the University of Alabama. He added so many pages that the scrapbook became more than two inches thick!

Then when he was 13, his knees felt sore as he walked home. After a doctor examined him, Bobby and his family were told that he had rheumatic fever. Rheumatic fever is an infection that can set in after someone has had strep throat. In the United States now, it is rare, but Bobby got it in 1943. It occurs mostly in children and results in inflammation of the joints and can cause heart problems.

Bobby had to stay in bed for many months, spending his days listening to radio reports about World War II. It took a long time, but he recovered and eventually made the high school football team.

When it came time to go to college, he enrolled at the University of Alabama. But Bobby, who was a quarterback, stood 5 foot 7 and weighed 165 pounds, and he soon realized he was too small to compete with much bigger players. So he transferred to Howard College in his hometown.

His teammates at Howard nicknamed him "Beebop" because he was full of energy and jumped around a lot.[1] After graduating, Bobby realized his football dream by becoming a coach. The pay for a young coach at a small school wasn't much, so he had to work extra jobs. He worked the late shift at a tobacco warehouse, where he would sometimes catch a nap atop the bales of tobacco leaves, and he also was a lifeguard. But at least he was doing what he always wanted to do—coach. He had to work the extra jobs, sure, but people were beginning to notice his name. Many coaches move every few years, hoping to win at one school so they can go on to a bigger one. And that's exactly what happened to Bobby, now known as Coach Bowden. In the late 1960s, West Virginia University hired him as an assistant coach. When the head coach left for another job, he told the school that Coach Bowden was the man to replace him. And in 1970, Bobby Bowden found himself as the head coach of the West Virginia Mountaineers.

In that first season, Coach Bowden learned an important lesson about not taking things for granted. His team was leading rival Pittsburgh Panthers 35–6 at halftime. When he brought his squad out of the locker room in the second half, he decided to play carefully and deliberately so they would not get beat. But Pittsburgh had other ideas because they marched down the field, time and again, wearing down Bowden's team. When the gun sounded, the final score was 36–35, and Pittsburgh had won.

Coach Bowden vowed never to let that type of loss happen again, so he worked even harder. He believed that you should never want to "win at all costs" and that preparing to win is most important.[2]

In his six years at West Virginia, he had only one losing season. Meanwhile, things weren't going so well down at Florida State University. The Seminoles—named after a tribe of American Indians—had won only four games in three seasons, and the school wanted to make a coaching change. Then one day in late 1975, Coach Bowden's phone rang. It was an official with Florida State, asking if he would be willing to move there to coach the team. When Coach Bowden said yes, it would be the final coaching job he ever accepted, but no one knew it then.

When he arrived in Tallahassee, where Florida State is located, he found that a high school team actually was attracting more fans than the college he was going to coach. The Seminoles had a losing season in Coach Bowden's first year as head coach, but it would be his last losing season. He stayed on at Florida State for 34 years and accomplished a rare feat for college football coaches, by winning more than 300 games.

There were many great games over the years that the Seminoles won with Bobby Bowden as their coach. Some are extra special. In 1993 and 1999, his Florida State teams won the national championship. But in 1999, an important game took place and not only for Coach Bowden but also for his entire family.

Coach and his wife, Ann, had six children. In fact, because he had sons who played and coached, the Bowdens were known as "the first family of college football."[3] One of his sons, Tommy, became the coach at Clemson University in South Carolina. The Clemson Tigers were in the same conference as Florida State. And on October 23, 1999, Florida State and Clemson met in a big game. It was the first time a father and son at large colleges had coached against each other. There was another reason why the game was so important: Coach Bowden was going after his 300th win. The teams played tough, and the Seminoles were losing for much of the game, but in the end, Florida State won, 17–14.

The victories meant a lot to Coach Bowden, but he prided himself on helping his players grow up to value more than just football. As a matter of fact, football was the fourth-most important thing in Coach Bowden's life, after God, family, and others around him. As a coach, he knew he had to be strict with players, but he remembered when to laugh. Once, when he was at West Virginia, the coaches and players were watching the film of a 20–0 loss. Coach Bowden became so mad he started yelling and walked out of the room, opening a door and slamming it behind him. There was silence. All of a sudden, the players heard a knock from the other side. It was Coach Bowden, who had walked into a closet; he had locked himself in. A player opened it, and he came back in the room—laughing.

When it came to preparing for a game, Coach Bowden became serious and worked hard and demanded that his assistant coaches did, too. He often would rise at 5 a.m. He and his coaches worked hard to plan for the Seminoles' upcoming opponent, and sometimes this meant using a trick play. That's when a team does something surprising to catch the other team off guard. He worked on trick plays back at Howard College, and he always knew they could be useful at the right moment. That moment came along in 1988, when he tried a play known as the "puntrooskie." Florida State and Clemson were tied, 21–21, with little time remaining. The Seminoles had the ball deep in their own territory, and it was fourth down. Many coaches would punt at this point, ensuring the game would end in a tie. So Bobby sent in his punter, and the teams lined up. The ball was hiked, but instead of the Florida State punter catching it, another player caught the ball and quickly sneaked it to a teammate between his legs without the Clemson players noticing. Then all the Seminole players ran to the right—except for one player, LeRoy Butler, who had the ball. He waited just a moment, and as players on both teams were running right, LeRoy went left and raced almost 80 yards. A Clemson player tackled him right before he crossed the goal line, but Florida State kicked a field goal and still won.

"The thing people don't know about Bobby is how smart he is," his friend Deacon Jones told a reporter once. "He has a mind like a steel bear trap."[4]

Because Coach Bowden demanded a lot from his players, he tried to set an example. He didn't drink, smoke, or curse. And even though he coached for so many years in Florida, his home state of Alabama held a special place in his heart. For years, he would return to meet friends and raise money for scholarships so needy students in Birmingham could attend college. Once, it looked like he had a chance to return to Alabama to be the head coach. The governor even called him about returning to coach at the school he idolized as a boy, but things didn't work out, and he stayed at Florida State.

He coached many players and tried to instill values that are important for all students. For instance, good habits, he believed, are "habit-forming" and "dependable." Also, he believed that "knowledge is power," and that people should never, ever quit learning.[5]

"Don't worry if you're not very wise. No one is born wise," Coach Bowden once wrote. "But you can learn to be wise. It just takes time . . . and sincere, diligent effort."[6]

People, like football players, can make mistakes. But when a mistake is made, a person should ask, "How could I have handled that situation better? What can I do differently next time that will lead to a more satisfying solution?"[7]

He also knew life could be tough sometimes. "Adversity will come," he wrote. "You must decide how you will face it."[8] Adversity, a state of hardship or misfortune, is something we all face at one time or another.

Casey Weldon, a great quarterback who played for Coach Bowden, once said, "You realize he's prepared you for life after football."[9]

Coach Bowden retired in 2009, so he has time to enjoy things he likes most—being around his family and reading military and religion books. He always remembers how fortunate he was to do what he loved.

"I just love to coach," he said. "I love to take a group of young men in the late summer and turn them into a team."[10]

Toward the end of his career, he summed his years in college football in a simple way: "I really feel like I was born to coach."[11]

Coach Bowden says:

- Coach Bowden's favorite books: "My inspiration growing up was my mother and father. My mother used to make me go to the local library and check out a book and read it, and when I finished it, go get another one and read it. Since then my hobby has been reading and playing golf. My favorite reading has been military history. I have read all the books I could find on Robert E. Lee and Stonewall Jackson. History was my major in college, and I love to read history books on American heroes of the past, its presidents and successful leaders. My one favorite book has been the Holy Bible, King James version. I have read and reread it through front to finish three times. Every time I read it is like I never read it before. I discover new facts each time. It is like God speaking to me. I went to Israel . . . and actually stood and walked on the same stones that Jesus and his disciples walked. It was inspiring and brought the Bible to life!"
- Coach's words of wisdom: "The best thing I've learned is you must be persistent if you wish to succeed. Never, never, never quit in the words of Churchill."
- Coach's main obstacle growing up: "I think the biggest obstacle I was faced with in growing up was lack of confidence. I had to keep reinforcing the thought that I am as good as anyone in what I do. This has not always come easy, especially after failure, which we all experience."
- "Remember, what you see and hear and *read* is what you become!"

Robert E. Lee (1807–1870) was the commander of the Confederate Army during the Civil War. Thomas Jonathan "Stonewall" Jackson (1824–1863) was a general who reported to Lee. Winston Churchill (1874–1965) was the prime minister of England during World War II.

3

DAVE BURBA, BASEBALL

An Ohio Homecoming

Can you imagine cheering for a team as a young boy and then growing up and playing for them? That's what happened with Dave Burba.

Dave was born in 1966 in Dayton, Ohio, but grew up about 25 miles away in Springfield. Like many good athletes, he played several sports and different positions. At Kenton Ridge High School, he was a tight end and punter in football, played basketball, and was a first baseman and third baseman on the baseball team. But he found his home as a pitcher.

"Dave was an all-around athlete," said his high school coach, Tom Randall. Dave also was growing; he turned out to be 6 foot 4 and more than 200 pounds—"a big strapping kid," coach Randall said.

Occasionally, Dave used to go to Riverfront Stadium, about 1 ½ hours away, to watch his favorite team, the Cincinnati Reds. Back then, the Reds were known as "The Big Red Machine." Many of the players on the team in the 1970s wound up in the Hall of Fame, including the great catcher Johnny Bench and a quick second baseman named Joe Morgan, who went on to become an announcer. Being named to the Baseball Hall of Fame is a great honor. It's located in Cooperstown, New York, and honors the best players with pictures, plaques, and artifacts. Dave had their pictures on his wall back home in Springfield.

When it came time to go to college, he wasn't recruited by many schools. His grades weren't the greatest, and he considered going to a small college for a while. But he really wanted to go to Ohio State

University, a large school in Columbus, the state's capital. Even though he wasn't offered a scholarship, he decided to try his luck and work hard to make the team.

"I wasn't the type of guy where everybody said 'This guy is going to be a first-rounder' or anything like that," Dave once told a reporter.[1]

So he might have been what is considered an "overachiever." He learned the value of a solid work ethic from his mother and father, who was a plumber. He worked hard, and "he had good control," Coach Randall said. "He actually got stronger after he left high school."[2]

Dave made the baseball team at Ohio State, a college known more for its football team. In 1987, the Seattle Mariners drafted him in the second round, high enough to show confidence in the young hurler from Ohio. But in baseball, teams often trade players, and Dave eventually was sent to the San Francisco Giants. But in 1995, another team showed interest in him, and they worked out a deal with San Francisco. It was the Cincinnati Reds! So Dave headed back to Ohio.

He pitched well for the Reds for several seasons. Then, in 1998, the team gave him great news: He was going to start on Opening Day. In baseball one of the best honors for a pitcher is to start the first game of the season because that's when all teams put their best pitchers on the mound, and the stadiums often are sold out. When he was young Dave had never attended Opening Day because he was in school. Then a funny thing happened. Just hours before the season began, the Reds had a change of heart. They worked out a last-second trade, and Dave was sent to the Cleveland Indians. The Indians had a young hitter named Sean Casey, who the Reds really wanted, but to get him, they had to trade their best pitcher. So Dave was on the move again; this time four hours to the north to play ball near Lake Erie. This body of water is one of the five freshwater Great Lakes in North America. You can remember their names by recalling the word "HOMES": Huron, Ontario, Michigan, Erie, and Superior.

About two months later, the Indians traveled to play Cincinnati in an interleague game. That's when teams from the American League and National League play each other during the season. The only other time that happens is the World Series. Dave learned it was his turn to pitch, except this time he was playing *against* the Reds. If he were nervous, he didn't show it. He won the game for Cleveland, who beat Cincinnati that day, 6–1. Not only did Dave earn the victory, he also hit a home run, which is a pretty rare feat for a pitcher.

He went on to pitch in more than 500 games before retiring in 2004. Throughout his career, he had a good reputation with his teammates, fans, and the media. In 1999, the writers who cover the Indians awarded Dave the team's "Good Guy Award," given to a person who is cooperative and professional. When he played in San Francisco, a group of fans started a cheering section in their hometown 200 miles away called the "su-BUR-BA-nites." He also donated autographed jerseys and batting gloves to his high school, Kenton Ridge, in Clark County, Ohio.

"It's where you come from and you want to give back," Dave once said.[3] His high school coach understands the importance of that statement. What Coach Randall remembers best about the "strapping kid" he coached was that he grew to be a "quality young man" and not just a good pitcher.

"The greatest thing about Dave is he still comes home and goes to his old grade school. Dave Burba never forgot where he came from."[4]

After Dave retired, he started coaching his son's Little League team. He liked it enough to go into coaching full-time, and in 2010, he became the pitching coach for the Tri-City Dust Devils, a minor league team in Pasco, Washington.

In recent years, Dave coached in the Colorado Rockies organization, helping their younger players learn the game.

"It's development, absolutely. That's what it's all about," he said. "Obviously, you want to teach them a winning recipe, but the end game is making them ready for the next level and more importantly for the big leagues. It's pride and satisfaction. It's about the accomplishment for the kid. Of course you take pride in helping in the process, but it's all about the kid actually following through, pursing his dream and achieving it."[5]

Just like Dave Burba.

Dave says:

- Dave's favorite book: "A book about Chuck Yeager and *Of Mice and Men*. The book about Chuck was interesting to me because I wanted to fly jets. *Of Mice and Men* I enjoyed because it was about an adventure of two guys trying to live a dream."
- Dave's advice for kids: "The most important thing I could advise kids on is get a good education. Pay attention in class and listen to what teachers and mentors have to say. I had to overcome bad study habits. My grades were very bad in high school. When I went to college I had to meet certain standards to be able to play baseball."
- Dave's inspiration: "My dad always inspired me when I was a young boy. He taught me a lot about doing the right thing."

Chuck Yeager (1923–2020) served in the Air Force as a fighter pilot during World War II. He also test-piloted planes, and became known for breaking air-speed records. Of Mice and Men *was written by John Stein-beck (1902–1968) and published in 1937. It takes place during the Great*

Depression, a difficult time in the early 1930s for many Americans. It tells the story of pals George and Lennie, who hope to work hard so someday they can have their own land to tend to rabbits. It's a story about loyalty and friendship.

4

TODD CHRISTENSEN, FOOTBALL

Big Player, Big Words

Fans sometimes consider professional athletes "dumb jocks" and that they just care about their sport and little else. When Todd Christensen came along, many people changed their thinking.

Todd, who was born in 1956, grew up loving sports. When he was six years old, he entered a track meet and won. By the time he was 10 he had earned dozens of track and field awards. But at home his parents emphasized learning. After all, his dad was a professor at the University of Oregon in Eugene, Oregon. His mom encouraged him to read about different subjects. When he became a football player, she would write him letters before games.

"My parents were always adamant that I not portray myself as a dumb jock," Todd once said.[1]

So he kept reading, and he worked out to stay in shape. On the Sheldon High School football team in Eugene, Todd was a standout who played both offense and defense. He earned All-State honors as a running back on offense and as a lineman on defense. It takes a lot of effort to play on "both sides of the ball," as it is called, because those players rarely get a chance to rest. When schools started recruiting Todd, they wanted him to play defense. All except for one school—Brigham Young University in Provo, Utah, more than 800 miles from his home. The school had 30 football scholarships, and Todd received the 30th. There were six fullbacks ranked ahead of him. All six suffered one injury or

another, and Todd got his chance. He gained a reputation as a running back who could catch the ball.

In 1978, professional teams started looking closely at Todd, and the Dallas Cowboys drafted him in the second round. The beginning of his professional career was a bumpy ride. He got injured, and he wasn't very happy when the Cowboys coaches told him they wanted to make him a tight end. The team cut him, and then he signed on with the New York Giants and played sparingly on special teams. Players on special teams are the ones who defend on kickoffs and punts. But he didn't stand out enough, and the Giants let him go. Other teams called but nothing worked out, and before long he returned to his wife and young son in Dallas. "By this point, my self-confidence was non-existent. I was getting rejected at every turn."[2] Then a chance came that would mark the real start of Todd's career.

The Oakland Raiders, known for their tough-guy image under colorful owner Al Davis, gave Todd a tryout, and they signed him. He played on special teams and found himself getting in games as a tight end. That position requires a player to be able to catch the ball, especially in crucial times during a game. Jim Murray, the great sports columnist for the *Los Angeles Times*, once wrote that a tight end must be "half-ape, half-antelope."[3] So Todd Christensen, who started as a running back in college, now found himself as a tight end on the rugged Raiders team. How good did he turn out to be? After being cut and rejected by several teams, he became the first tight end in the National Football League to catch 80 passes in four straight seasons. He was named to the Pro Bowl—the all-star game of the league's best players—five consecutive times. He became, as author Tom Needham wrote, "nearly unstoppable."[4] He was gaining a reputation as a classic overachiever, someone who exceeds what people think he or she can do. In fact, he became so good, a coach once said "he could catch a burning log."[5]

Todd wasn't the only Raider playing well. The whole team was great. They went to the Super Bowl twice in the 1980s, as the Oakland Raiders in 1981 and the Los Angeles Raiders in 1984, and won both times.

Through his career, he continued to read. As much as people marveled at his play on the field, they also noticed something about him off the field: his vocabulary. This wasn't a guy who would grunt at reporters or speak in clichés about winning the big game. This was a person who had read books, and he liked to quote from them. It was not uncommon for Todd to mention historic figures from the past. He would refer to writers like William Shakespeare, Henry David Thoreau, and Herman Melville. Shakespeare was an English writer who wrote many famous plays, some funny and some tragic, including *Romeo and Juliet*. Thoreau was a poet, and Melville was a novelist who wrote *Moby-Dick*, a famous book about a whale. Both were Americans who lived in the nineteenth century. Sometimes Todd quoted a former world leader, like Benjamin Disraeli—a British prime minister in the latter part of the nineteenth century—or a scholar named Desiderius Erasmus. He was a Dutch scholar who lived in the fifteenth and sixteenth centuries. Todd never shied away from talking about the people he had read about or using large words to describe things. One writer even said he sounded more like a professor than a football player. In the days leading to the Super Bowl, the final game of the season that determines the world champion, reporters come from all over to talk to the players and coaches to hear their thoughts on the big game. What did Todd want to talk about before the 1984 game? The fact that he was reading *The Life and Times of Benjamin Franklin* and a book about Mohandas Gandhi. Franklin was a famous US statesman, author and scientist in the eighteenth century, and Gandhi was a peaceful Hindu spiritual leader who was assassinated in 1948.

When Todd's playing days ended in 1988, he quickly found a second career that seemed only natural for him: He became a broadcaster. He worked on a show with Roy Firestone called *SportsLook*. He helped host an early reality show called *American Gladiators*, where competitors wearing protective gear would compete in obstacle courses and strength challenges. He announced volleyball and track, his first sport, and—of course—football. Like all announcers, some people liked his style and others didn't. One man who found Todd a fresh voice in the announcers' booth wrote a letter to a Milwaukee newspaper and said "Christensen is a bright spot in an otherwise boring bevy of broadcasters."[6]

The Raiders from Todd Christensen's era are remembered as a tough lot, winners who played hard. The 6 foot 3, 230-pound tight end who started out as a running back is remembered as a key part of that history. A few years after he retired, the Raiders drafted a tight end named Ricky Dudley. He knew he would be compared to Todd and previous Raiders, and he didn't mind.

"I remember Todd Christensen, some of the great plays they made, some of the great things they did," Dudley said.[7]

In 2013, Todd underwent surgery for a liver transplant. Sadly, there were complications and he died. He was 57.

Todd says:

- Todd's words of wisdom: "At the age of seven, I became mesmerized with a football game on television. It was an old black and
  white Hoffman television with a giant green tube and screen so
  everything was, well, black, white, or gray. The Cleveland Browns
  were playing the New York Giants, and I was mesmerized by the

rhythm of the sport, the physicality, and the athleticism. My father purchased for me a rubber football and kicking tee which I took with me constantly after school from August through January. I would practice by myself, envisioning great feats and imagining myself being the great Jim Brown."

- "But I have been fortunate to have my inspiration at the dinner table. My father and mother were hard-working people of integrity that I looked up to. The Bible, the Book of Mormon, biographies of Malcolm X, Abraham Lincoln, and Mickey Mantle were among the books that influenced me positively. I was blessed to grow up in Eugene, Oregon, and blessed to be in the Ned and June Christensen family."

The Book of Mormon *is a sacred collection of holy readings for Latter-day Saints. Malcolm X (1925–1965) was born Malcolm Little but changed his name and became a minister in a religious group called Nation of Islam during the Civil Rights movement. Abraham Lincoln (1809–1865) was the 16th president of the United States. Both Malcolm X and Abraham Lincoln were assassinated by gunmen 100 years apart. Mickey Mantle (1931–1995) was a great baseball player for the New York Yankees. Even though he hurt his knee badly early in his career, he played 18 seasons in the Major Leagues and batted .298 with 536 home runs. Eugene is a city in the western part of Oregon about 60 miles from the Pacific Ocean.*

5

FRANK DEFORD, SPORTSWRITING

A Born Storyteller

Like many kids growing up in the 1940s and 1950s, Frank Deford was always around sports in some way. He read about them in the local newspaper in his hometown of Baltimore, Maryland. A tall boy, he played basketball, starting out on a team in a recreation league called the Baltimore Hawks. But there was something else Frank loved to do when he was young: Write.

He once said, "I've been a natural writer since age 8."[1] At age 13, he won a national short-story writing contest. He was the editor of his high school paper. The printer happened to be close to a famous horse track called Pimlico, and Frank would drop off the stories after school and scoot over to the track to watch the races. He was enjoying the two things he loved most: sports and writing. He might not have known it then, but he would stay involved in those two subjects for many years and become one of the greatest sportswriters ever.

He remembered his childhood fondly, once saying, "I had a mother and father who loved me, great brothers and an extended family. It was absolutely idyllic. It's hard for me to imagine better."[2] "Idyllic" means a place that has a natural charm to it.

When it came time to go to college, Deford chose Princeton University in New Jersey. There he played basketball and edited the school paper, the *Daily Princetonian*, and the humor magazine, *The Tiger*. But his playing career ended when a coach told him, "You write basketball

better than you play it."[3] So Deford concentrated on his writing, but he never lost his love of sports. After college he landed a job with a relatively new magazine called *Sports Illustrated*. That was 1962, right around the time that television was bringing more games and more sports into people's living rooms. He was young, the magazine was in its early stages, and times were a little different for writers and athletes. Now, many professional athletes make millions of dollars and don't have to work in the off-season, but back then, they had to have jobs when they weren't playing, and they often didn't make as much as some of the writers covering them. "I started my career at a time when writers and athletes could be friends," he once said. "I was lucky."[4]

He also was lucky to have attended what many people consider the greatest football game ever, the 1958 NFL Championship. The Baltimore Colts—Frank's favorite team, quarterbacked by his favorite player, Johnny Unitas—defeated the New York Giants. By the time he became an established writer, he had the chance to travel the world and cover different sports in many countries. One of his most memorable was a 1980 tennis match at Wimbledon in England. Wimbledon is one of the most prestigious tennis tournaments of the year. A Swedish player named Bjorn Borg defeated John McEnroe, an outspoken American, in a hard-fought match, and Frank was there to witness it—and to write about it.

There were many athletes who he watched, interviewed, and wrote about. The most inspiring to him was a champion tennis player and civil-rights activist named Arthur Ashe, who became friends with Frank before Ashe died at the age of 49. There were other great players, too, whose careers were taking place on courts or on fields as Frank was becoming a proficient writer—meaning he was performing well in his craft. Wilt Chamberlain, for instance, was one of the first great "big men" in basketball, but he was someone who Frank wasn't wild about at first. Eventually, they got to know each other and became good friends. In 1962, Chamberlain—who was taller than 7 feet—scored 100 points in a single game; that record still stands. Then there was Bill Russell, who Frank admired as a tremendous team player when he starred with the Boston Celtics.

Watching great players do well or teams battle in a challenging game or match, stirs a passion in many people, and he is no different. "I can still get juiced up," Frank told a reporter. "When I see something good, I can get absolutely involved. The saying goes that there's no cheering in the press box. But you should be cheering in your heart, or you won't be a good sportswriter."[5]

Frank's career blossomed. He was known not only for his writing but also for his distinctive, thin mustache, which he wore for years, and the well-dressed, dapper (neatly dressed) manner with which he carried himself. (He once even received a "Looking Great Award" from a fashion writer.) He also was starting to write books, both fiction and nonfiction. Then came a big change: He decided to leave *Sports Illustrated* to become the editor for a special publication called *The National*, which started in 1990. This was a big deal, because although *Sports Illustrated* was a magazine that came out once a week, *The National* was going to be published almost every day. And like *Sports Illustrated*, *The National* hired some of the greatest writers and editors in the country. When the owner was looking for someone to run the paper, he chose Frank. Unfortunately, *The National* encountered some business problems and closed less than two years after it started.

It seemed like Frank had everything, but in fact there was a time when things were much less than perfect. He and his wife, Carol, had two children—a son, Christian, and a daughter, Alex. Alex was a beautiful little girl, but when she was little she was always sick, coughing a lot. Doctors examined her and diagnosed her condition as cystic fibrosis, a disease that affects about 1 in 2,000 babies. It especially weakens the lungs by drawing bacteria into them. And it hurts girls more than it does boys. When Alex was little, the Deford family had to do special massaging exercises on Alex to make her feel better, and she spent a lot of time in the hospital. They had to crush awful-tasting medicine in applesauce for her. And even though she knew she was sick, she rarely complained. She was a beautiful girl who had lots of friends and enjoyed many things that other kids did. She loved dancing, the color pink, and listening to the famous opera singer, Beverly Sills. She dreamed of visiting Hawaii and liked to laugh a lot, especially at a wacky British comedian on television named Benny Hill. And she loved a famous racehorse named Ruffian, who her father covered. Ruffian was a filly—a female horse—who was a great champion in the 1970s.

Alex died in 1980. Frank did not want his daughter to be forgotten, and he hoped to raise awareness about the disease, so he wrote a book called *Alex: The Life of a Child*. He said writing it to let people know about cystic fibrosis was "probably the best thing I've done."[6]

After the book came out, Frank kept writing about sports. And he was honored for it. He won the US Sportswriter of the Year award six times. One writer once began a story about him like this: "Frank Deford has become arguably America's greatest living sportswriter by understanding that the best sportswriting is about much more than sports." It was true; he liked writing about the people who played the games so fans could learn about the players and coaches they followed. And he didn't mind *how* the stories were told. In 1980, he started doing commentaries for National Public Radio. Some made you think about a special event or moment in sports; some made you sad; and others made you laugh. He recorded more than 2,000 for listeners to hear.

"I always wanted to be a story-teller," he once said.[7] Sometimes it is in print and sometimes it is on the radio or TV, but telling stories is what Frank was always about.

Frank died in 2017. He was 78.

Frank says:

- Frank's favorite books: "There were two books I especially loved growing up. *The Adventures of Robin Hood*, by Howard Pyle, was a classic at the time. Robin is one of the most intriguing and delightful characters in literature, and, reading about him as a boy, I dreamed about being one of his Merry Men myself."

- "*Johnny Tremain*, by Esther Forbes, is a novel about a young boy who works in Paul Revere's silver-making shop at the time the Revolution begins in Boston. Johnny gets involved in all the secret goings-on and made me wish I could've been there with him as America began."

- "Both of these books heightened my interest in history, and they're both just terrific yarns that encouraged me to want to be a writer."

- Frank's words of wisdom: "It is so important, as you grow up, to try to balance two things. First, try to find something that you love and try to follow that passion. But, as the same time, realize your limits. The American Dream has sometimes been distorted in a way that can hurt young people. Yes, we all have a chance in this country, but, no, we cannot be assured of success just because we seek something—and no matter how hard we try."

- "So, be prepared to fail but then be ready to steer your hopes in another direction. You must learn to temper ambition with reality so that you can find the right, happy place for your talents."

6

TONY DUNGY, FOOTBALL

Calm and in Control

On January 21, 2007, things didn't look too good for Coach Tony Dungy's Indianapolis Colts. They were losing 21–7 against the tough New England Patriots. And it was a big game, the conference championship. The winner would go on to the Super Bowl. Few people among the 57,433 in the sold-out RCA Dome, the Colts' home field, could have thought their team had a chance.

But Coach Dungy—known for never getting rattled—did not panic. He knew he had a great quarterback in Peyton Manning, and he trusted in his team's preparation for the game. Teams have a specific game plan each week based on their opponent's strengths and weaknesses. But the Colts were different. Their game plan was more complicated. They relied on the quarterback looking quickly at the defense and figuring out which play to call. Manning then would bark out the play in codes to his teammates.

The game turned into what is sometimes called a "slugfest." When the Patriots scored, the Colts would come back and tie the game. Back and forth it went. Then, with about two minutes remaining, Indianapolis found itself down by three points. They had to go about 80 yards. With controlled, precise passes, Manning drove his team down the field until they were just a few yards from the end zone. That's when he handed the ball to running back Joseph Addai, who shot straight through the middle behind great blocking and scored a touchdown. Tony Dungy was headed

to his first Super Bowl as a coach. Professional football's championship game is now held on a Sunday in February. The first one was in 1967 when the Green Bay Packers beat the Kansas City Chiefs.

Coach Dungy is known as "one of the most respected coaches in the game."[1] He earned that respect by studying as hard as he could, whether it was in the classroom or in preparation for a game.

Coach Dungy attended high school in his hometown of Jackson, Michigan, a city of about 80 miles west of Detroit and named for the seventh president of the United States, Andrew Jackson. He was good in several sports, including football. One day a man named Tom Moore came from the University of Minnesota to recruit him, and he told the young player how his team operated on offense. We'll give you a few plays, he told the star quarterback, and you go out, look at the defense, and call the one you want. Tony liked what he heard and went to Minnesota. Years later, when his team faced the New England Patriots in that big game in 2007, the man who had recruited him to college was right by his side as an assistant coach for the Colts.

It took many years, hard work, and several coaching jobs for Tony to go from college at Minnesota to leading the Colts to the biggest game of all, the Super Bowl. He started out playing professionally with the Pittsburgh Steelers, but his playing career was average. As good as Tony was on the field, he was a much better coach. And people realized it. His coach at Pittsburgh, Chuck Noll, saw how smart he was. At age 28, Coach Dungy became the first African American defensive coordinator in the National Football League (NFL). To this day, Coach Dungy considers Noll one of the most important people in his life because of the encouragement he received.

Tony also had a lot of support from his family growing up. His father and mother valued education for all their kids. In fact, his siblings grew up to be a doctor, a nurse, and a dentist. He concentrated on playing sports and was a pretty well-behaved kid. He rarely was unruly or raised his voice. Although many coaches yell and go crazy on the sidelines, Tony never did. He always stayed calm, never yelling or panicking. Players respect a coach who doesn't scream at them all the time. "He's one of those guys who, when he talks, people listen," a fellow coach, Monte Kiffin, once said. "Some people talk too much. Tony chooses his words carefully."[2]

Even back in high school, Tony kept his wits about him. His junior year, his team went 4–5. Instead of making excuses, he buckled down and led his Parkside High team to an 8–1 record his senior year.

When he became an assistant coach in the NFL, he concentrated on being the best one he could be. And in 1996, he became one of the youngest head coaches ever when the Tampa Bay Buccaneers hired him. The Buccaneers had recorded losing seasons in 17 of their 20 years of existence. Coach Dungy was determined to change that. In his six years leading the team, Tampa Bay had only one losing season.

But coaches are always on the move, and Tampa Bay's executives decided they wanted to try a new coach. Coach Dungy wasn't without a job for long. In 2002, the Colts hired him. The team performed well, and in 2007 found themselves in that battle with New England. No team had ever come back from 18 points down in a conference championship, but the Colts did it. Two weeks later, Coach Dungy—in his usual calm manner—led his team to a 29–17 victory over the Chicago Bears in the Super Bowl. The Colts had become world champions. The game was important for another reason. The Bears were led by Lovie Smith, a good friend of Coach Dungy. It was the first time two African American coaches had faced each other in the Super Bowl.

Speaking to reporters after the game, Coach Dungy said "I'm happy, but winning it is not the most important thing in the world, because there are other things like working in your community, doing things the right way and taking care of your family."[3]

Coach Dungy remains as calm off the field as he does on the sidelines. He is a religious man, and his belief in God remains a constant force in his life. His faith has seen him through good times—like winning the Super Bowl—and difficult ones, like when his son died in 2005.

Two seasons after his team's Super Bowl victory, Coach Dungy announced he would retire. True to his word, he was interested in many things besides football. He enjoys listening to jazz music and fishing for walleye, a freshwater fish with large eyes. He has written several books, helping others understand the importance of being a mentor and encouraging children. He is involved with All-Pro Dad, a group that encourages men all over the country to be better fathers for their children. In fact, in 2017, Tony promoted the Daddy Read to Me Summer Challenge through the organization.

In 2016, Tony Dungy was enshrined in the Pro Football Hall of Fame, a great honor. When coaches and players spoke of him, it wasn't just about the games he won as a coach; it was the type of man he was that impressed them. One of those coaches, Mike Tomlin of the Pittsburgh Steelers, remembered his first day as an assistant in Tampa Bay for Coach Dungy. He walked into Tony's office and saw the coach's son playing video games on the big projection screen the coaches used to watch game film. Tony always wanted his coaches to have a life outside of football and to remember the importance of family.

"In an instant, it showed me how he balances who he is and what he does. It left an imprint on me," Tomlin said.[4]

Tony went into broadcasting as a football commentator and is known as an insightful analyst, someone who helps viewers understand why teams do the things they do on the field. He was nominated for a Sports Emmy Award for his work. And Dungy speaks on camera the same way he used to coach: calm and in control.

Coach Dungy says:

- Coach's favorite book: "Favorite book early on, *Green Eggs and Ham* (by Theodor Geisel). When I got to junior high I enjoyed reading sports biographies. As a teenager *Roots* by Alex Haley had a big impact on me. I didn't read as much as I should have. I definitely advise kids to read, dream and work hard to achieve those dreams."
- Coach's words of wisdom: "The best advice I got was to keep my eyes on the Lord and follow Christ, because he is actually the one who makes those dreams come true."

Theodor Seuss "Ted" Geisel (1904–1991), who was known as "Dr. Seuss," wrote children's books that rhymed. Green Eggs and Ham *came out in 1960. He also wrote a famous holiday book,* How the Grinch Stole Christmas. *Alex Haley (1921–1992) wrote the novel* Roots, *which came out in 1976 and follows an African man named Kunta Kinte, who was sold into slavery in the 18th century.*

7

MIKE ERUZIONE, HOCKEY

Believing in Miracles

Many kids dream of scoring the winning point or shot in a game; it's only natural. Mike Eruzione experienced that dream in real life. Only the game wasn't a big one just for him. It was important for the entire country.

Mike grew up in Winthrop, Massachusetts, not far from Boston's Logan Airport. When he was a boy, he learned to skate by wearing his sister's figure skates—complete with pompons—and occasionally played hockey on a friend's pool that was frozen over during the winter. He attended Boston University, where he led his team to a string of hockey conference championships and never missed a game. After college, he was good enough to play hockey in the Minor Leagues and was named the International League's American-born rookie of the year while playing for Toledo. At this time, coaches and officials were assembling the US hockey team to compete in the 1980 Olympics. It's an honor to be named to any Olympic team, but this year's was extra special: The United States was the host country. The Winter Games would be held in Lake Placid, New York, not far from Canada.

The world was a little different in 1980. The US economy wasn't doing so well, and several dozen Americans were being held captive in Iran. Meanwhile, the United States was going through a time known as the Cold War with the Soviet Union. The nations weren't at war physical-

ly, but tensions between them were like two bullies who eyed each other from a distance on the playground.

So when the US hockey team was named, Americans became excited, hoping the team could win a medal. But everyone knew how tough the Soviets were. How good were they? A year previously, in an exhibition game against the best professional players in the National Hockey League, the Soviets skated to a 6–0 win. Their teams had won four consecutive Olympic gold medals. In fact, in an exhibition just days before the Lake Placid games, the Soviets beat the Americans, 10–3. The Soviets were the top-ranked team in the world. No one, it seemed, expected the Americans to beat them.

But the US coach, Herb Brooks, believed in his players. Brooks was a longtime respected college coach, though many people forget he was the last player cut when he tried out for the 1960 Olympic team. It was the last time the Americans had won an Olympic gold medal in hockey. His goal for the 1980 team was to create a well-conditioned team that could pass precisely. Players came from Minnesota to Massachusetts, and he worked them endlessly for six months. One of the drills players had to endure were "Herbies," which were essentially sprints on skates. The players were mostly college players, not professional stars, and their average age was 22.

The Americans played Sweden first, and the game ended in a tie. Then came wins against Czechoslovakia and Norway. They skated past Romania and then beat West Germany. The only thing left was the medal round, where the best teams advance, and the showdown was set: It would be the mighty Soviets, who had not lost a game in the Olympics, against the upstart Americans.

It was below freezing outside the arena on February 22, 1980. Inside, fans packed in for the big game. When the players walked in to the locker room they found hundreds of telegrams from all over. The normally talkative team was quiet, knowing how big of a game they were about to play. Mike said it felt like he was in church, it was so quiet.

But things became a bit louder when they filed out of the locker room and skated on the rink. "When we stepped onto the ice it started. 'USA! USA! USA!' I felt as if I were 10 feet off the ground," he said.[1]

The Soviets jumped to a 1–0 lead, but the Americans fought back and tied the game. From that point, the teams traded goals. Every time the Soviets scored, the Americans answered. One of the most exciting came when Mark Johnson shot the puck into the goal and tied the game 2–2—with one second remaining in the first period!

"When a team that's supposed to have no chance suddenly sees that victory is possible, it becomes a game of emotion," Mike said.[2]

The teams battled on. The Soviets fired shot after shot on goalie Jim Craig, a teammate of Eruzione's from college. But the Americans didn't give up. With about 10 minutes remaining, the score was tied 3–3. Earlier, the Soviet coach had pulled his starting goalie from the game in frustration. It was a surprise move, because Vladislav Tretiak was known as one of the best goaltenders in the world. Buzz Schneider of the US team shot the puck up the ice, along the boards, where players battled for it. It kicked out to the middle of the ice, where Eruzione—the captain of the team and one of the oldest players, at 25—had skated in from the left. He caught the puck on the blade of his stick about 25 feet from the Soviet goal. He twisted his stick and fired a wrist shot, which is when a player flicks the puck in, as opposed to a slap shot, where the player slams the puck hard. It quickly sailed past one defender and then by surprised goalie Vladimir Myshkin, who stumbled backward. The goal had put the Americans up, 4–3.

"What I saw was the net," Mike said in a book he wrote. "The back of the net suddenly bulged out, punched back by something. It took a moment to realize it. But then I saw the fans behind the goal leaping up out of their seats, hands in the air, and I knew. The roar was deafening. My legs took over, and I just started running on my skates, high-stepping in the corner like some crazy drum major at a halftime show."[3]

But there was still time remaining, and the Soviets did not let up. They slammed every shot they could at the Americans, but Craig held firm. When the buzzer went off, the arena went crazy. The Americans, on their home soil, had defeated the best team in the world. Al Michaels, broadcaster for the game on television, screamed what is now one of the most famous announcer calls about any game: "Do you believe in miracles? Yes!" People chanted "USA, USA!" over and over. Fans waved flags, big and small.

Outside in the Olympic Village, fireworks exploded. Later, Mike said how special the win against the Soviets was. "It was the greatest moment in sports, and I'll tell you why. . . . Our win was national." It wasn't about pride for just one team or one city, he was saying, it was for the entire country.[4]

One of the interesting facts about the game is even now many people think it was for the gold medal. The Americans actually would win that two days later by beating Finland 4–2. When the medal ceremony was held in the arena, it was team captain Eruzione who stood on the platform, singing every word of the National Anthem. But when the anthem ended, he immediately waved to his teammates, who were standing on the ice. "C'mon, c'mon!" he yelled. He was telling them to join him—and they did, huddling together, as a team.

"I've always told people even if we didn't win, we would still have these friendships, the bond. It was a great moment for me and my teammates, and it touched so many people in positive ways," Mike said.[5]

Many of the players went on to great professional careers. But not Mike. Even though he was good, he wanted to go out on top, so he retired.

After the game, all sorts of offers came in for him to speak to groups of business people. He would be paid thousands of dollars just to talk for a few minutes to companies. His post-Olympic career included working at his alma mater. That's the school or college that a person has attended.

He coached some high school hockey. He gives speeches all over the country because people still want to hear about the game. He occasionally works as a hockey analyst on television, and he is involved in many charity events.

Even today, more than 30 years later, people still talk about the game, and movies have been made about it, like Disney's *Miracle* in 2004.

"It never gets tiring," Mike once said. "It's something I would never trade for. I had the experience of not just being an Olympic athlete, but of touching so many lives at the same time. That's pretty good."[6]

After the Olympics, he returned to Winthrop, his hometown in Massachusetts right on the Atlantic Coast, where he still lives, and where he still recalls the 1980 Olympics fondly.

"I always felt pride putting on the USA sweater, playing for my country. But this was something I'd never imagined."[7]

Mike says:

- Mike's favorite books: "I always read sports books—baseball, football—it seems that is what I was playing so it made sense to read them."
- Mike's words of wisdom: "Work hard, make the right choices, respect people and yourselves. Always believe in your dreams."
- "Hard work can achieve anything."
- Mike's inspiration: "My parents inspired me by teaching me about the right values in life—realizing that in order to be the best you have to work at it. It's not easy. It's your life; you decide how you want to live it."

8

GERRY FAUST, FOOTBALL
A Dream Fulfilled

When Gerry Faust was in grade school back in the 1940s, he would ride his bike to football practice in Dayton, Ohio, with his cleats tied over the handlebars, helmet on his head, and a smile on his face. He would whistle the Notre Dame fight song. Gerry told everyone his dream: To grow up to be the football coach at the famed university.

Gerry lived for football. His dad was a longtime coach at Dayton Chaminade High School, the same school attended by actor Martin Sheen. At first, Gerry's dad, nicknamed "Fuzzy," cut his small, 103-pound son from the team. But Gerry worked hard, made the team, and starred as quarterback his junior and senior years. He was good enough to earn a scholarship to the University of Dayton, where he graduated in 1958.

After his playing days ended, Gerry started off to achieve his dream. He began coaching football at Moeller High School, a Catholic school in Cincinnati. In 1963, the first year Moeller had a varsity team, Gerry guided the squad to a 9–1 record. As the years went by it seemed Moeller never had a bad team. From 1963 to 1980, Gerry—known as Mr. Faust to his players—led Moeller to an astonishing 174–17–2 record. They shut out opponents 90 times! They won many regional and state championships and were known throughout the country as a powerhouse. Gerry had made a name for himself.

Over the years, more than 250 players at Moeller earned college scholarships. Several went on to Notre Dame, which made Gerry proud. Then
in 1980, Gerry's wife Marlene suggested they go to the annual spring
football game at Notre Dame. While Gerry was there he went to a special,
sacred place called the Grotto. He lit a candle and prayed that someday
his dream of becoming a football coach at Notre Dame would come true.

Gerry went back to Moeller and continued coaching. It was another
good season for the team. He had a busy life. In addition to having a
family, Coach Faust taught math at the school, and he worked hard to
support the football team in ways other than coaching. He and the other
coaches built a weight room for the team, and he personally sold ads in

the program for football games. That's known as being a jack-of-all-trades, a term for a person who can do many kinds of work. He kept the players focused, making sure they concentrated on their studies and their practices, leaving their many recruiting letters unopened until after the season. Gerry also prayed every day in front of a statue of the Blessed Mother, who is important to Catholics.

Then one day Gerry got a surprise call from a Notre Dame official. The football coach was considering stepping down to spend more time with his wife, who was ill. Would Gerry be interested in talking about the possibility of becoming coach?

Gerry and his family were happy at Moeller, but this was his dream! For a long time he told his bosses at Moeller the only coaching job he would ever take would be Notre Dame's. Now the school was interested in him, a high school coach, and he could hardly believe it. Gerry was offered the job, but for a while he couldn't tell anyone because an official announcement hadn't been made. But he needed to talk to someone to make sure he was doing the right thing. He couldn't even tell his wife. So he told the one person whose opinion he valued very much, the man he considered the best coach he ever knew, his father. Fuzzy told him if he got the chance he should take the position. Gerry got the job, and he began to live his dream.

Notre Dame is a special school with a lot of history. It is run by priests and is known to be a well-respected academic university. The school is in South Bend, Indiana, less than 100 miles east of Chicago and only a few miles from Lake Michigan. For a few years, the College Football Hall of Fame also was in South Bend. Notre Dame's history is well-known to fans. The Fighting Irish, as they have been known since 1927, won their first national championship in 1925, and always fielded strong teams. They had dozens of All-Americans over the years, and many stories about their football players became legendary. A famous sportswriter, Grantland Rice, was so impressed after seeing the Irish beat Army that he nicknamed four of their players the "Four Horsemen." It gave a Notre Dame student working to promote the team an idea. He had a picture taken of the four players on horses. Then he distributed the photo to as many newspaper writers as possible. The story—and the team—became even more popular. In those days, the Irish had a coach, Knute Rockne, who helped popularize the forward pass, now commonly used at all levels of football. Even the school's fight song, the "Notre Dame Victory

March," is famous; it is one of the four most popular songs in US history (along with "White Christmas," "God Bless America," and "The Star Spangled Banner.") And overlooking the entire campus is a giant gold domed building. To this day, the football team wears simple, all-gold helmets, just like the top of the famed building.

Gerry knew about all this, and he realized he was stepping into a big job. One of the first things he did was borrow a friend's library collection about Notre Dame—19 books! He wanted to learn as much as he could. One of the things he found is that Notre Dame fans are demanding. The job as football coach there is known as one coaches want very much, but it's also one of the toughest. When Coach Faust arrived at Notre Dame, some people called his hiring "the bold experiment."[1] That was because it is rare for a high school coach to jump to a university like Notre Dame. Usually, coaches work as an assistant at a college to prove themselves, and then they hope to land a head job. Not Gerry. He loved Notre Dame, and the school loved him, and he was hired.

Things started well, with a big win over Louisiana State University in September 1981. But they didn't stay that way for long. There were differences, to be sure. For one, Gerry was used to coaching high school football, where games are 48 minutes. In college, they are 60. And Notre Dame started losing—not by much, but a loss is a loss. By the time Coach Faust left, his teams had lost 26 games over five years. The problem was, 15 of those losses were by a touchdown or less. Against some schools he had success, but many fans and the media thought he should have beaten others, like Air Force, more often.

Gerry loved Notre Dame. He enjoyed being around the people and praying at the Grotto. (He once even said he would have become a priest if not a football coach.) He was popular, too, because he was so likeable. At one point, he received 50 to 100 letters a day. Gerry had a way with those around him. You always knew when you were talking to Gerry on the phone because of his distinctive, raspy voice. And he was full of energy. He liked to greet people quickly with a "hi, hi, hi!"[2] Gerry had, some people, said, "unbreakable optimism."[3] That means he always expected the best possible outcome. A sports editor in Ohio named Frank Corsoe once said Coach Faust "is one of the most genuine human beings I have had the privilege of meeting. Five minutes talking with him makes me a better person."[4]

But being likeable doesn't mean a school will keep you as coach. An encyclopedia on Notre Dame football sums up his career at the school by stating, "His five years in that position were impressive for a man with no collegiate experience—but not impressive enough for the Fighting Irish."[5] Even though Gerry had a winning record at Notre Dame, 30–26–1, his teams never won more than seven games in a season.

When it was announced that Notre Dame wasn't going to bring back Coach Faust, he received many supportive letters. More than 3,500 arrived from all over the world! "It's too bad that coaches are judged on their win-loss record," wrote one of his former players, Wally Kleine, who said Coach Faust stood "for everything a man should be—honest, loving, caring, devoted (and) hard-working."[6] Coach appreciated that letter, as he did the many others because one of the things he values most is loyalty. It wasn't just letters that Gerry received. When other schools found out Notre Dame wasn't going to keep Coach Faust, offers of coaching jobs began pouring in. Gerry and Marlene had a lot to think about, but he wasn't afraid of the future. "When you are not afraid to fail in life, you'll succeed," he once wrote. "When you're not afraid to take something on even though the odds are against you, you are going to emerge a success in one way or another."[7]

So they considered the many offers. They almost went to Rice University in Houston, Texas, but decided on the University of Akron. It would be in their home state, close to family and friends. Akron was not as high profile a school as Notre Dame, but it posed a different challenge. Officials at the university, which is just south of Cleveland near Lake Erie, wanted to join a bigger division in college football. It would mean better competition, but it would be tough. The Akron Zips hoped Coach Faust would be their man.

Being at Akron made the coach feel like he was back at Moeller. Unlike Notre Dame, with many people working in support roles, Gerry had to do a lot of things by himself, like replacing floors and redoing offices. He found the going rough, and after nine years with the Zips, he retired—sort of. He had such a positive outlook, he went to work fundraising for the university.

Coach's personality was so outgoing that for years he was sought after by many groups to speak. At one point, he was giving 150 speeches a year. And through it all, Coach Faust has few regrets. "I've been very lucky," he once said.[8]

Moeller, the high school where Gerry had a lot of success, honored him in 2007 with the naming of the Gerry Faust Sports Complex.

Even though he stayed at his dream job for only five years, he was content. "It would have been easy to dwell on the negative. But life is full of ups and downs. What matters is how we handle what we're dealt. How we react determines whether or not we survive and are happy."[9]

Coach Faust says:

- Coach Faust's favorite book: "My favorite book is *The Golden Dream*, a book I helped write with Steve Love. It's a story about having a dream and reaching that dream and living the dream for five years, then deciding that it was time to give up the dream because you weren't accomplishing the results that were necessary but be able to handle that setback as other setbacks you have in life because of having the three most important ingredients in life: Faith in God, love your faith; family, all you need is one family member; and friends, all you need is one friend. Having those three ingredients in life you can be happy and productive in your life."

9

TONY GRANATO, HOCKEY

Basement Dreams

Tony Granato played hockey on rinks all over the world as a member of the US Olympic team. He competed in the National Hockey League (NHL) for 13 years, skating with the sport's best players in arenas in the United States and Canada. But the first "arena" where he played was the smallest one and the players were the most important people in his life: It was his basement in suburban Chicago, with his siblings.

Using a puck made from tissue and masking tape, and taping the carpet with red and blue lines, the Granato clan split into teams and played floor hockey for hours downstairs in their home in Downers Grove, Illinois. They painted "USA" on goalie masks. When they weren't playing, they watched a tape of *Miracle on Ice*, a film about the 1980 Olympics in which the US hockey team stunned the Soviets. They watched the tape so much it wore out.

Of course, the basement wasn't the only place Tony—the oldest of six—and his siblings learned to play. In fact, Tony's first experience with the sport came when he was two years old, when his father took him to Chicago Stadium to see his beloved Blackhawks. The stadium had the feel of a rickety old barn. Tony, his father said, would be "mesmerized by the action." When he was six, his parents brought him to rinks where he swooshed happily around the ice.[1] When he got older, he and his siblings skated in a makeshift rink in their back yard in the winter, and they would

come in for dinner still wearing skates. His idol was Stan Mikita, a great player on the Blackhawks.

It seemed the family was always playing hockey or going to games together. Vacations were spent driving to clinics in other cities. One writer called the Granatos the "first family of hockey."[2] Tony's brother, Don, played in college and later went into coaching. Brother Rob got involved in a roller-hockey league in the Chicago suburbs. The siblings even lent their name to a team for the Disabled Athletes Floor Hockey League, the Downers Grove Granatos. Sister Cammi was a pioneer in women's hockey, becoming the captain on the first US women's Olympic team in 1998. The team did not lose a game and won the gold medal.

When it came time to go to college, Tony—who played forward—chose the University of Wisconsin, a hockey powerhouse about two hours from the family's home. In 1987, he was a finalist for the Hobey Baker Award, the annual honor that goes to the best college player. It is hockey's version of college football's Heisman Trophy. He was drafted in the sixth round, the 120th pick, by the New York Rangers. It is uncommon for players to be drafted below that mark to make it in the NHL, but Tony did. After playing on the US Olympic team in 1988, it looked like he was off to a great career. He even made the NHL's All-Rookie team in 1988–1989. Tony was described as a "little dynamo" in one of his hometown newspapers, the *Chicago Tribune*.[3] It was a good description of a player who was 5 foot 10 and about 185 pounds—not as big as most players in the NHL. Another paper once described him as being a "roaming hornets' nest" on the ice, meaning he always went after pucks aggressively.[4]

But not everyone's career, or life, is without ups and downs. In Tony's case, he had to endure injuries, including a serious one in the NHL. First, when he was a young boy, his parents noticed his left leg looked crooked while he was learning to skate. Doctors found he had a hereditary problem, but they fixed him up, and his career took off. Something that is hereditary comes from one's ancestors or means being born with something. Then, during his junior year in college, he broke his collarbone when he tried to stop a puck with his hand. He had reached out and was checked by a defender, sandwiching his shoulder between the boards and the other player. He missed several weeks of games. While playing professionally with the Los Angeles Kings a few years later, Tony was treated for an inflamed disc in his back. And in one game when he was with the San Jose Sharks, a puck flew up and hit him in the face, breaking his jaw. But all of these injuries were nothing compared to what he went through in 1996.

The Kings were playing the Hartford Whalers, and Tony was flying down the ice as fast as he could. He and a Whaler were racing side by side, and their momentum carried them so fast they smashed into the boards. Tony hit his head and got up slowly. "At first, I thought it was just another hit. I'd be shaken up, see some stars, then shake it off like I would any other hit," he told a reporter.[5] But it wasn't any other hit. Even though he played again two days later, he wasn't feeling right. He started having headaches, and he had problems remembering things. A doctor examined him and diagnosed him with an intercranial hematoma. A hematoma is an area in the body that fills with blood. In Tony's case, a mass of abnormal blood vessels had formed in his left temporal lobe, which is the part of the brain that controls memory. The odd thing is, doctors believed it had been there since Tony was born. Whether it was there for a long time or triggered by the hit into the boards didn't matter; it was "potentially life-threatening," as one doctor put it, and needed to come out.[6] Tony said later the worst part was the night before, when the headaches intensified. On Valentine's Day 1996, Tony underwent a four-hour surgery. His family had flown in from all over the country to be with him, and friends sent cards and fruit baskets. But a question remained: Would Tony be OK, and would he be able to play again?

After the season, Tony—who now had a six-inch scar in his head—went home to rest and think about his future. He had to have follow-up visits with doctors, who told Tony he could continue to play, if he wanted to—and he definitely did. He signed a contract with the San Jose Sharks. In his second game of the season, Tony scored a goal. Then another and one more. He had scored a hat trick, the name given to three goals in one game. He also assisted on a teammate's goal. In hockey, a goal and an assist count in a player's statistics as points. Tony had scored four points in one game, an impressive total, but especially important to him since he had come back from serious surgery.

But something even more impressive was about to happen. Each year, hockey writers vote on a player who shows "perseverance, sportsmanship and dedication to hockey." Perseverance is so important. It means the holding of a course of action, belief, or purpose without giving way. The award is called the Bill Masterton Award, named for a player who died after hitting his head on the ice during a game in 1968. In 1997, the writers voted to honor Tony Granato with the award. Not only had Tony come back from brain surgery, but he had also made the All-Star team.

Every player's career comes to an end at some point, and in 2001, after 13 seasons as an NHL player, Tony decided to hang up his skates. However, he didn't leave the game of hockey entirely. Rob Blake, a former teammate of Tony's, once said, "As a player, if there was a time the team needed someone to get up and speak, Tony usually was the guy who got up and spoke."[7] So it was no surprise when the Colorado Avalanche hired him to be a coach. He led the team to a 104–78–17 record over three seasons as head coach. A big moment in his coaching career came in 2003, when Tony brought his Avalanche team to his hometown, Chicago, to face the Blackhawks. Colorado won, 5–4. Tony continued coaching and eventually moved on to Pittsburgh, where he became an assistant with the Penguins. He also coached with Detroit and Team USA. In 2016, the University of Wisconsin, where he had attended, named Tony head coach.

"From the moment I left campus, always in the back of my mind and in my heart was 'Please someday end back up in Madison.' To come back and be part of the program again, I can't tell you what it means to me. Badger hockey, even though I've been out of the program for a long time, has never left my heart. I've followed it, I've cheered for it."[8]

When Tony was in college he once said, "I always dreamed about playing college hockey and maybe professional someday. Every player dreams it that way. I'm just glad it worked out."[9] The dream that started in his parents' basement did come true for Tony.

Tony says:

- Tony's words of wisdom: "Follow your dreams and set your life goals high. With hard work, persistence and a good plan you can reach your goals."
- Tony's inspiration: "My parents were who inspired me. Great foundation and values of hard work, family, love, opportunity, faith and commitment. These are the values that my parents have instilled in all of us."
- "Obstacles, many injuries and lots of people telling me I'd never make it were great motivation."
- Tony's favorite books: "Books (by) John Wooden and John C. Maxwell."

John Wooden (1910–2010) was the successful, long-time basketball coach at University of California, Los Angeles. His teams won many championships and dominated the sport for years. John C. Maxwell (1947–) is a pastor and professional speaker who writes often on the qualities of leadership.

10

TIM GREEN, FOOTBALL

A Busy Man

Sportscaster Bob Costas once said, "One is considered fortunate to be blessed with either brains or brawn; Tim Green has been blessed with both."[1]

Tim Green started out as an athlete but soon became a lot more. He never wants to stop learning new things. Tim grew up in Liverpool, New York, near Syracuse, where snowfall reaches about 115 inches a year. Like a lot of boys, he played Little League baseball. In high school, he wrestled (and even became a state champ) and played football. When it came time to go to college, he could have gone to any one of several schools, but he chose to stay home and attend Syracuse University.

On the field, Tim played defense, and one of his main jobs was to get to the quarterback. He had more than 45 sacks in college, the most ever by any Syracuse player. At one point, local businesses started a "sack fund" for charity. Every time Tim broke through the line and tackled the quarterback, the businesses would donate money to the March of Dimes. He led his team to a berth in the 1985 Cherry Bowl in Michigan, the first postseason game for Syracuse in six years. Tim was one of the stars of the team, and he knew he had a chance to play professionally. So he took advantage of a new rule the National Collegiate Athletic Association (NCAA) had just made. If a player became seriously injured he would not be able to play professionally and would miss out on making a lot of money. So the NCAA decided players could insure themselves, the way

people insure cars and houses. Tim had his dad look into it, and they took out a policy.

Tim wasn't just smart about how to handle himself on the field. Off the field, he had another love: books. A professor named Judith Weissman saw in Tim a person who wanted to learn, and she helped him by becoming his mentor. Tim studied English literature and was an A student with a 3.83 grade-point average. He also became a Rhodes scholar finalist. One of the most prestigious academic awards, the Rhodes scholarship allows just 32 American college students per year a chance to study in England. It is competitive and a great honor. When he graduated, he and another student were valedictorians of their class.

It seemed every time Tim explored some new interest, he did well. In college, he took a martial-arts class. He worked hard at it and ended up earning a black belt.

When the National Football League (NFL) draft came in 1986, Tim was selected by the Atlanta Falcons, where he played eight seasons and continued two of his favorite pursuits: hunting down opposing ball carriers and reading. Tim rarely was without a book. Even in the locker room, amid the uniforms and the towels and rolls of tape, Tim always kept a book close by. He would read works by many writers, including Charles Dickens, an English novelist (1812–1870) who wrote *A Christmas Carol*, among other notable books.

Tim had another passion: writing. "I was an avid reader as a kid. I loved books. Because of that I always wanted to write," he said.[2]

Growing up in Tim's house meant books were everywhere. "My parents really got me hooked on reading as a kid. We made a weekly trip to the library. They were just voracious readers, and they instilled that habit in me, reading books instead of watching TV."[3] Someone who is voracious is eager to consume in great amounts.

Tim began to get as serious about his writing as he was about football. "When I was a little kid," he once said, "I had two goals—to play football in the NFL and to be a published author."[4] Like anything else, writing takes practice. But Tim didn't have much time to write; he was spending many hours running drills on the field, lifting weights, or attending meetings. NFL teams have many meetings. Players watch hours and hours of film on their next opponent. They hear coaches talk over and over about where each player should be on each play and what they should expect. Preparing for the next game in football means going over things repeatedly because practice makes players better. But Tim sometimes found his mind wandering. So he started to jot notes about story ideas in the margins of his playbook. Carefully, he would tear off the tiny scraps of paper and stash them away. Late at night, he wrote fiction. His novels used football as the backdrop.

Then, several years after his career ended, he wrote a book called *The Dark Side of the Game*. This book was different for several reasons. It was nonfiction, for one. It was about life as a football player, something Tim obviously knew well. Writers are told to write what they know, and Tim certainly knew football. He took the reader into the locker room. He described what his 6 foot 2, 245-pound body went through physically in a game. What Deion Sanders was like as a teammate, what referees talk about on the field, and how it feels to get tackled on grass versus artificial turf. He talked about what players go through at the "combines"—where college players are tested and poked and prodded by coaches and doctors. They are evaluated for their speed, strength, intelligence—even their teeth are checked out! And how training camp is so grueling that the favorite part of the day for players is when they can nap. He wrote about fun things, too, like how players bond when rookies are made to sing the fight songs from their colleges. Tim had a knack for using words wisely and made life on and off the field very vivid for readers. For example, he wrote:

> Getting to the NFL is like climbing Mt. Everest, there's a distinct pleasure in just the knowledge that you're one of the few who ever made it.[5]
>
> When you run out onto the field of an NFL stadium, that energy from the crowd surges into your veins . . . (and) feels like you might just get lifted right up off your feet and zip off into the sky.[6]

Mt. Everest is a huge mountain on the border of the countries Nepal and Tibet. It contains the highest peak in the world at more than 29,000 feet.

One of the most important messages in the book is that although statistics are important, a fan should always remember to enjoy the beauty of the game. The reader comes to know Tim through his words and learns how much Tim loves a challenge. "It's the most grueling, challenging sport there is. Brute strength, cunning speed, gut-wrenching endurance are all wrapped up into one fast-paced hard-hitting uproar."[7]

But Tim wasn't content to just sit back and write. He had other things to do. He had married Illyssa, his girlfriend from college, and they had started a family. He also had gone to law school, and he graduated with honors. Through his career he wrote columns for newspapers and did commentary on radio. He is comfortable on television; one writer says he looks similar to the actors Tom Cruise and Christopher Reeve. After his career ended with the Atlanta Falcons in 1993, he worked in television more. He even hosted a show called *BattleBots*, where remote-controlled robots clashed in an obstacle course. But Tim also embarked on another project, an important one. Like many people who are adopted, Tim wondered about his biological mother, so he set out to find her. It took him six years and a lot of research, but he did it. In 1997, he wrote a book about the experience, *A Man and his Mother: An Adopted Son's Search*. And because adoption is important to Tim, he cohosted a television show called *Find My Family* to help other people like him.

Meanwhile, Tim kept writing. "I'm in the habit of being busy, being productive. Every day is different, and writing is an important part of every day."[8] Tim had conquered fiction and nonfiction for adults. Then one day an editor read one of his books and thought his style of writing would be perfect for younger readers. Tim liked the idea, so he started writing for kids. He wrote *Football Genius*, about a 12-year-old boy who has the ability to forecast plays on the field before they happen. *Best of the Best* is about a boy and his pals who are competing for a baseball championship, but the boy, Josh, is bothered by his parents splitting up.

Another passion for Tim was speaking to school kids about the importance of reading. He once estimated he has spoken to more than 70,000 children in his lifetime! His message is clear: "Books are weight-lifting for your brain."[9] Tim has written more than three dozen books.

Tim gives 100 percent to his projects and always keeps busy. "He's always on the move, nonstop energy, more so than anyone I've ever worked with," said Kenny Albert, one of Tim's television colleagues. "He's one of the nicest, most genuine people I've ever met, but he is a perfectionist."[10]

Syracuse University honored Tim by naming an award after him. The Tim Green Award goes to the best defensive lineman each year. In 2019, Syracuse retired Tim's jersey, number 72. He was the first defensive player to have his jersey retired at the school.

Through all his projects, television work, and writing, Time remained in the place he loved best: Upstate New York, where he was raised and went to college. He also spent time coaching football and wrestling.

Life was going well for Tim, but a few years ago he started noticing problems with his hands. It was getting difficult to do simple things, like using his nail clippers or taking the lid off a jar. He thought it was aches and pains left over from his football-playing days. He went to a doctor who told him that he had ALS. ALS stands for amyotrophic lateral sclerosis, a disease that destroys nerves that move muscles in your body. It's also known as Lou Gehrig's disease because a great baseball player named Lou Gehrig had the then little-known disease many years ago. No one knows how most people get the disease.

Tim and his family decided to try to help others fight the disease. They created a fundraising campaign called "Tackle ALS" to raise money for doctors and researchers.

Despite having ALS, Tim cherishes the time he has with his family. Steve Kroft, a man on a television show called *60 Minutes*, interviewed Tim back in 1996, just a few years after his career ended. Then, more than 20 years later, he interviewed him again about his life and dealing with the disease.

"Some people would say, you know, 'Tim, God bless you,'" Tim told the interviewer. "And I'd say, 'He already has.'"[11]
Tim says:

- Tim's favorite books: "My favorite book growing up was *The Count of Monte Cristo* but the series I liked best and what really got me into reading was The Hardy Boys."
- Tim's words of wisdom: "I think the most valuable lesson I would share is to be kind and respectful to others. We all want people to be kind to us, and to respect us. Many people struggle to get others to respect them, but it's simply: you get what you give. Be kind, kindness comes back. Be respectful, respect is yours."
- "There were many obstacles I had to overcome, injuries, and falling short of many goals. The best lesson of sports is perseverance. That's what I love so much about football. It's a game of getting back up. Life will always knock us down but in sports we learn that you just keep getting up."

The Count of Monte Cristo *is a classic adventure tale written by Alexandre Dumas (1802–1870). The story, set in the 1800s, is about a man who is falsely accused of a crime and goes to prison. He escapes and seeks those who imprisoned him. The Hardy Boys follows two teenage brothers, Frank and Joe Hardy, who are amateur detectives and solve crimes.*

11

JANET GUTHRIE, AUTO RACING

Speedy Trailblazer

From the time she was a little girl, Janet Guthrie wanted to go fast.

But before she ever stepped into a race car and zipped around a track, she had another passion: She wanted to fly a plane. Flying was in her blood. Her dad flew and managed an airport in Iowa, where Janet was born. She was a quick learner; it took her only two hours to master riding a bike. As a girl growing up in the 1940s and 1950s, she loved to build model planes. After her family moved to Florida, she even got a chance to skydive once, jumping out of a plane her father piloted.

The area where the Guthries lived posed a few special challenges. Janet and her family had to be wary of wildfires, hordes of mosquitoes, poisonous snakes, and even wild panthers.

Janet attended college, majored in physics at the University of Michigan, and continued her love of flying. Physics is the science of matter and energy and how they relate. She also received her commercial pilot's license. When she graduated, she accepted a job with an aviation firm in New York. She loved flying so much she even considered being an astronaut.

One day, she was offered the chance to be part owner of a plane. She went home to think over the deal. Then she came on a small advertisement in the newspaper: A Jaguar was for sale. The sleek automobile seemed to call out to Janet, "Drive me, drive me!" It was at this moment

she made a life-changing decision, one she would never forget. She bought the car and not the plane.

Not long after, Janet came across what was known as a gymkhana. It was a race on a course set up with pylons for drivers to maneuver around; hit one, and you were penalized. A pylon is a structure marking the turning point in a race. It often is a red cone. At first Janet watched, but it wasn't long before she decided to dive into a race. She did well enough to feel confident to move on to another racing competition, called a hill climb. A hill climb is exactly like it sounds: You race up a mountainside. Again, Janet did well, and racing was now in her blood.

In one early race she finished third and received a silver cup, which she still uses as a sugar bowl. Even though Janet was not making much money at her job, she poured every cent she possibly could into racing. What started as a hobby quickly turned into a passion. "Nothing that I know of is anything like it," she says in her autobiography. [1]

But Janet knew cars break down, especially ones that are being driven hard around tracks. So she learned to do the maintenance herself. With limited tools, she replaced the brakes on her car. She even rebuilt an engine. Racing can be dangerous, going 150 or even 200 miles per hour around a track, so drivers and their mechanics want to keep cars in the best shape possible. But the most dangerous thing that ever happened to Janet actually took place when the car wasn't moving at all. It happened when she was in a friend's garage. When she smacked part of the car with a mallet, a sharp piece of metal broke loose and cut Janet above the eye. After she stopped the bleeding, she went back to work on the car.

These were lean times for Janet. Often, she had to set up her own mini-garage right in the back of her station wagon, which was her nonracing car. Not having enough money, the station wagon not only was her garage but also her bed; she slept there instead of a motel the night before a race. But Janet stuck with it. After all, she had come to love racing with all her heart.

Then something happened that became as important as the decision she had made years previously to buy a car instead of a plane. One night, after working in a friend's garage, she went home and found a message on her answering machine. A man named Rolla Vollstedt called and said something amazing: "Please call me about a possible ride in the Indianapolis 500."[2] Janet hardly could believe it.

The Indy 500 was the country's premier racing event. Racers speed 200 laps around the famed track in the middle of Indiana. No woman had ever competed in it. When Janet started racing, there weren't many women in the sport—and there still aren't. There were women who raced here and there, but none had made it to the annual Memorial Day weekend race in Indianapolis. A Frenchwoman named Camille du Gast is believed to be the first serious competitor in the sport, back in the early part of the

1900s. Camille entered the Paris–Berlin race in 1901. Despite organizers making her start last, she finished 33rd of more than 100 racers. In 1903, she drove in the Paris–Bordeaux race and showed not only talent in driving a race car but good sportsmanship. When she came upon a racer who had crashed she helped him and stayed with him until an ambulance arrived. Like du Gast, Janet Guthrie was a pioneer in racing.

Rolla Vollstedt turned out to be true to his word. Despite many men objecting to a woman competing in "their" sport, Rolla thought the time was right for Janet, who had worked hard to get to where she was. She also was racing in National Association for Stock Car Auto Racing (NASCAR) events, and now she hoped to be in the greatest race of all.

NASCAR and Indy car racing are similar in that they both are about driving fast, and usually on oval tracks. But there are many differences. The cars have different specifications, which means engines come in different sizes. Plus there are other rules and regulations that govern each form of racing. Indy racing is considered "open wheel" racing, whereas NASCAR is not. Depending on schedules, some drivers like to race in both events—with different cars, of course. Another factor drivers must consider is sponsorship. Companies pay drivers' teams money to have their company name put on race cars. This pays the bills. When you see a race on television, this is why product names are plastered all over the cars. When Janet was racing, her sponsors included Kelly Girl, an employment agency, and Texaco.

In 1977, not only did she become the first woman to compete in the Daytona 500, but she was also named top rookie in the race. But when the call from Rolla came, the idea of entering the Indianapolis 500 started to evolve from a dream into reality.

The Indy 500 is hugely popular, drawing fans from all over. It started in 1911. It attracts about 350,000 fans to the 2.5-mile track each year. It's more than just a race; it's a whole weekend of festivities, including a parade and the traditional singing of "Back Home Again in Indiana." Cars can go the length of a football field in less than one second. But before racers can line up in rows of three on the track, they have to qualify. That means to make the field of 33 race cars, drivers have to go through laps in the days leading up to the race and be clocked as one of the fastest times. The goal is to get the pole position, the inside spot on the front row. In her qualifying attempt for the 1977 race, Janet managed to hit speeds just under 190 mph! She earned a spot in the ninth row.

Janet enjoyed keeping a journal of her thoughts and things that happened to her throughout her life. It made her a better writer. In her autobiography, she wrote this about her experiences on the track in Indianapolis:

> It was like the beauty of dry shocks of corn in the farmed fields and the black leafless branches under the wintry blue sky. The empty stands were skeletal. . . . Only in one's imagination could the Speedway be fleshed out . . . the screaming cars, the colors, the heart of summer . . . the swirling flags, the crowds. [3]

Through all the qualifying and practice runs, and through all the work her team had done on her car, Janet had to endure many comments from men who did not want her in the race. Years ago, many people said women weren't strong enough to handle a race car, that they didn't have enough endurance, or could not handle the sport emotionally. People said the same things about long-distance women runners, and plenty of women have proven them wrong. Janet shrugged off the comments as best she could. One old guard at the track used to yell and shake a rubber chicken at Janet. But when she qualified, he sent her a dozen roses—and the chicken—saying he was wrong. A couple of men once even called out to Janet that they hoped she would crash. She won over many fans by being professional and showing she knew cars and how to race them.

Not all men opposed Janet. A reporter asked the great driver Tom Sneva who he felt most comfortable with on the track, and he mentioned A. J. Foyt and Janet. "They know their equipment and know how to drive."

Janet raced in the Indy 500 for three consecutive years, 1977, 1978, and 1979. The 1978 race was her best. She had competed once and knew what to expect. "Putting a car in the field at the Indianapolis 500 for the first time . . . had seemed like climbing Mt. Everest. It was the challenge of a lifetime, one that many great drivers had failed to achieve. But now, a year later . . . my head was out of the clouds, and what I wanted was to win the thing." [4]

But obstacles arose before the race. First, she needed a car and a sponsor. That took some doing, but she managed both. Her team didn't have a garage at the race. It took a lot of poking around, but they finally found one. A garage close to the track is important. Race cars don't just go fast without constant tinkering. Teams of mechanics have to adjust the car every time the driver stops. They adjust again and again, always seeking more speed.

Then, two days before the race, Janet was asked to play in a charity tennis tournament. During a match, she tripped and landed on her right wrist. A doctor soon confirmed the news: It was broken. A driver's right wrist is important because that's used to shift gears. When a Texaco official called, worried that she wouldn't be able to drive, she put him at ease—even though she wasn't sure herself. The fact was Janet could steer, but shifting gears remained a problem, though. She couldn't take a pill to dull the pain because her senses would not be as sharp, and when you're driving close to 200 mph, you need to have a clear head. So right before the race a doctor gave her an injection with enough medicine to help her wrist.

When Janet lined up at the start of the race, she did what she always did. She looked around to see who was in front and next to her. She had to be aware of who jumped to a fast start and who was slower at the beginning. Janet herself was considered a cautious starter. Soon, other challenges cropped up. Her racing suit was sagging over her eyes, making her vision difficult. But it was not as though she would have a red light to stop and adjust. She had to soldier on. Race-car drivers also have to contend with the temperature. If it is hot for people in the stands, it's much worse behind the wheel on the track. Janet's car—known as a Wildcat—also was just a little too short for her legs, so her feet were crammed in very tight.

Drivers also have to deal with what is known as the "g-force." The "g" means gravitational, and when a race-car driver is turning a corner at a high speed, it can feel like hundreds of pounds of pressure are pushing up against them.

The race wore on with veteran drivers Al Unser, Sneva, Gordon Johncock, Bobby Unser, Foyt, and others remaining just seconds ahead of Janet, who was driving 185 to 186 mph. She was close to George Snider's car, the two of them zooming around while trying to gain on the other. Finally, with less than a lap to go, their cars entered turn two, and Janet shot by George. She finished a respectable ninth, her best finish in the great race. It would be the best finish by a woman for 27 years.

"The woman drove 500 miles with a broken wrist. I don't know if I could have done it," Johncock said after the race.[5]

Janet Guthrie retired a few years later. One writer named her to the all-time field of the 33 most important Indy 500 racers. She said for years the biggest challenge for women racers is gaining sponsorship because without a sponsor, drivers can't enter a race. Her driving suit and helmet are in the Smithsonian, a massive museum complex in Washington, DC, so they are preserved for all to see and to remind us that she was the first woman to compete in the Indy 500.

And in 2021, it was announced Hilary Swank would play Janet in a movie about her life.

Janet says:

- Janet's favorite books: "Let me begin by quoting from my autobiography, *Janet Guthrie: A Life at Full Throttle*—'For most of my childhood, our single biggest treat was a trip to the public library. Oh, the riches there! . . . The very scent of the place was thrilling: mossy, stone-damp, saturated with the fragrance of thousands of books. Every week I checked out the maximum number of books— five, I think—devoured them, and came back next time for five more.'"

- "'Mostly I sought out adventure stories. . . . The imagined liberty of action was what appealed. Best of all were flying stories, especially from the distant past.'"

- Janet's words of wisdom: "Later on, flying was my first obsession. I soloed at 16, and had a commercial pilot's license and flight instructor's rating by the time I graduated from college. Books had enabled me to imagine what this would be like, and the reality was even better. Racing came after that."

- "I would say that the path to success lies in following your obsession, but you must build on your own particular strengths. For example it would be useless for me to think of *Dancing with the Stars* because I never could move in time with the music!"

- "As I also said in my book, 'Not everyone wants to drive race cars, but for each person the right challenge is out there, the challenge that is just the right size, the challenge that will evoke the best that a person can be.'"

12

LOU HOLTZ, FOOTBALL

The Upbeat "Do Right" Coach

If someone met Lou Holtz on the street, the last thing they would think of is football. He is thin, wears glasses, and talks with a lisp. And he wasn't a good player when he played. But boy, could he coach.

Lou was born in 1937 in Follansbee, West Virginia, close to where the Mountain State converges with Ohio and Pennsylvania, an area known for steel mining. When he was young, his family moved a few miles up the road to East Liverpool, Ohio.

"I was smaller than everybody else, people made fun of me, I had a terrible lisp, but you learn to handle that," he said years later. "You go through several stages of life, and the one stage you go through is childhood, where you learn that not everybody likes you, you aren't the biggest, the fastest, the strongest, the smartest, but you learn to handle that. You learn to find ways to succeed, and you have to keep trying until you find a way to get accepted, and then that carries you into life."[1]

Lou was right; he wasn't any of those things growing up. But he found a way to succeed.

Lou grew up poor. He had only one change of clothes, and he got a paper route to earn a few dollars. Lou's family lived in a tiny house. He had to share the same bedroom with his sister and his parents, and the bathroom had only a toilet. "I may have been poor, but the lessons my parents taught me were priceless. They taught me that life is about making choices. Wherever you are good or bad, don't blame anyone else."[2]

He followed sports—his idol was baseball star Ted Williams because the Boston Red Sox slugger had served in two wars and was a great ballplayer—but football was Lou's favorite. When he was in grade school, his uncle Lou coached the football team, and young Lou admired his uncle and desperately wanted to play. One day, he got in a game on defense, and the opposing halfback came rushing through the line—right at him. Lou froze. He missed his opportunity for a tackle and felt bad about it. He promised himself then he would never quit on a play again.

Lou always tried to stay positive through anything that was happening in his life. His friends called him "Sunshine" because of his upbeat attitude. He made the high school team, but unlike many stars who had stellar careers when they were young, Lou was average at best. And his grades were not impressive. Then one day, Wade Watts, his coach, asked for a meeting with Lou and his parents. Lou was surprised and thought he had done something wrong. His coach then dropped a bombshell on the family: "I think," he told them, "Lou should go to college and become a coach."[3] The coach had seen something in Lou, and the young football-loving kid never forgot it. When Lou became a big-time coach years later, not only did he invite Coach Watts to games, but he also let him ride on the team bus.

So Lou decided to go to Kent State University in northeast Ohio. Right before classes began, he was in a grocery store and heard two women talking. One told the other she was surprised Mrs. Holtz was "wasting her money" to send her son to college.[4] Lou was devastated. He knew he wasn't the best student, but he was hurt by the comment. Instead of believing the women, he decided to use the experience as motivation. So Lou went to college, studied hard, and played football—but he played sparingly. In the spring practice game, about a year before he was to graduate, Lou hurt his knee. It was bad enough for him to go to the hospital for surgery. By the time the leg got better, the season was over, and Lou was finished playing football. But he wasn't finished with the sport entirely. He got a job coaching freshmen at a nearby high school, showing guys who were bigger than him how to tackle and block and where to be on the field. He didn't wear pads, but he didn't care. He *had* to show them the proper ways to play. It would be the beginning of a career.

Coaches change jobs and move all the time. Each decision they make can affect the rest of their career, if they want to move on to bigger schools. Lou, now a young man, was dating a girl named Beth, and he proposed. He also had two job offers: He could move on to the University of Iowa and be a graduate assistant coach, or go to Conneaut High School in Ohio as an assistant. He chose Conneaut. He figured he and Beth would settle down in Ohio. But Beth said no. So Lou, hurt and confused, decided to get as far away as he could, and went to Iowa. The funny part of the story is that Beth eventually said yes, and they were married. But at this point, Lou found himself stuck in the farmlands of east-central Iowa. He worked hard. He did what the head coach wanted, running errands and coaching. From there Lou landed other assistant coaching jobs at different colleges, including Ohio State. The Ohio State Buckeyes had a famous head coach named Woody Hayes, whose teams were always competitive. Lou's coaching on a good team got him noticed. Schools saw he had moved up the coaching ranks and done a good job everywhere he went. Finally, he got a call, from the College of William & Mary in Virginia. Now, it was Lou's time to become a head coach. The team played hard for Coach Holtz, and they made it to the Tangerine Bowl in 1970.

Next stop: North Carolina State. The North Carolina State Wolfpack were known more for basketball in the Atlantic Coast Conference, and they had struggled on the gridiron. Lou jumped into his job headfirst, made them forget about losing, and they started winning. He led them to four consecutive bowl games. Those are special college football games featuring the best teams after the regular season. In doing so he caught the eye of the owner of the New York Jets. Coach Holtz didn't really want to coach the Jets at first. After all, he was happy where he was. His coaching career was going well. Off the field, he and Beth had started a family. They enjoyed playing bridge—a card game for four people—with other couples in their spare time. Raising a family and setting a good example was important to Lou, who used to teach the value of money to his children by taking them out to dinner and letting them each guess the price of the meal. Whoever guessed closest won a prize: a dollar.

But the idea to coach professionally was enticing, and the owner made such a compelling case that Lou couldn't resist. Besides, the Jets had their great quarterback, Joe Namath, who Lou had met and tried to recruit when he was at Iowa. Well, Joe and Lou got along great, but the team didn't do well. Years later, Coach Holtz admits jumping to the pros was the worst mistake of his life. "You have to be a confident person to admit you fouled up," he said.[5] But sometimes a failure turns into opportunity. The University of Arkansas snatched up Coach Holtz, and he was off to Fayetteville, in the northwest corner of the state, which was fine for Lou and Beth, who didn't like cold weather much.

Lou immediately got his Razorback team on the winning path. They won 10 games and were headed to the Orange Bowl in Miami. Everything looked great. Then, right before Coach Holtz and the team were to travel to Miami, his phone rang. A police officer told him three of his players were in trouble. After the players were questioned, the police decided not to pursue charges. Throughout his career, Coach Holtz always told his teams something simple but important: Do right. The players, in his mind, didn't do right. So even though a lot of people disagreed with him, Coach Holtz suspended the players from the season's biggest game. But football is a team sport, and the Razorbacks went on to beat Oklahoma, 31–6.

After several seasons in Arkansas, Coach Holtz received a surprise: He was fired. No one was more shocked than he was. But again, Lou didn't get down. It just meant a door was opening somewhere, and that door was in Minnesota. Lou called an important meeting with his family—by now he and Beth had two sons and two daughters—and considered all their options. Should they move north? Yes, they decided, and it was on to cold weather of the Big Ten Conference. As he always did, Lou turned around a lackluster Minnesota team, and again, by the second year, they landed in a bowl game. He never would have had the opportunity to succeed in Minnesota had he not been fired in Arkansas. Even though he was upset at the time, it worked out. "You never know when bad things are intended to lead you in good directions," he once wrote.[6]

But Coach Holtz did something then that no other coach had ever done. When he sat down with his family to consider taking the job, Lou had a sudden thought about his future. Deep down, he always wanted to coach at Notre Dame. He talked many times in interviews about attending St. Aloysius grade school as a boy and hearing the Notre Dame fight song several times a day. So he told the officials at Minnesota he would accept the job on one condition: Should the Notre Dame coaching job ever be offered to him, and if he had taken Minnesota to a bowl game, he would be free to leave. Minnesota officials reluctantly agreed. Two years later, Lou Holtz was true to his word: He had taken the Golden Gophers to a bowl game. And guess which job had opened up at the same time? Lou had become one of the best coaches in the country, and Notre Dame knew it. Their search for a head coach did not last long. "This is the happiest day of my professional career," he said when he was named coach of the Fighting Irish.[7]

He quickly took charge of the football program. He worked his team on conditioning. It was not uncommon for the slight, feisty man to clutch a player's face mask to show him what had to be done on the field. They listened. And when a couple of players missed a team meeting, Coach Holtz used his "do right" rules and suspended them for a big game. They came together as a team and began winning game after game, and when the national championship rolled around in 1989, it was Lou Holtz leading his Fighting Irish onto the field. Notre Dame beat West Virginia, 34–21, and finished the season 13–0 as the nation's best team. At one point over two seasons, the Irish had a 23-game winning streak, the longest ever for the school with the rich football history.

Lou retired after the 1996 season and went into broadcasting. But the urge to coach gnawed at him, and he wound up at South Carolina. The funny thing is that South Carolina had been one of Coach Holtz' early stops as an assistant. He had been fired and, at the time, didn't know what to do. So he sat down and wrote 108 goals to accomplish in his life. He wanted to meet the president. He wanted to skydive. He hoped to travel. He told himself he would learn magic tricks and how to juggle. By the time he was much older, he had accomplished most of the list.

Here was a coach who had experienced the highs of coaching (he won a national championship) and the lows (he was fired from several jobs) but never got down. "There may not be a more determined man than Lou Holtz," said Frank Stams, one of his former players.[8] When Lou got to South Carolina, the school was coming off a horrible season, and he struggled his first year, trying to turn around the Gamecocks. They didn't win a game. He slowly started getting the players to understand that a team is a family. And like he had done at every head-coaching stop, he guided them in a bowl in his second year. South Carolina went 8–4 in what became the greatest turnaround in college football history.

Lou finally retired for good after the 2004 season and demonstrated three qualities that television network people love about former coaches: First, he was successful. He had taken six different teams to bowl games. And he had four different teams finish in the top 25. Second, he loved to talk. Lou learned how to be a public speaker back when he was a young graduate assistant in Iowa. The head coach told him to speak to a group of business people, but he never told them Lou was the substitute. Lou had to win over the crowd—and he did, with humor. That's the third thing television people love: Someone who can tell a joke when they have to. When a reporter once asked him how he felt about fans throwing oranges on the field after his Arkansas team was invited to the Orange Bowl, he quipped: "Thank God we didn't get invited to the Gator Bowl."[9]

"You know, I could talk forever," he once said.[10] And he got his chance on ESPN, where he gave "pep talks" and told viewers about what teams have to do to win games. After all, it's what he did for many years.
Coach Holtz says:

- Coach's favorite book: "When I was in the third grade at St. Aloysius, I was the poorest reader in our class and that was OK with me. During the summer I became a sports fanatic; I started to read the sports page from front to back. While I struggled initially, by the time school started in the fall I was the best reader in our class."
- "By learning to read that summer, little did I realize this would prove to be an invaluable asset to me in the future. The books I read were primarily from the library as our family was quite poor and we couldn't afford to buy them. My favorite book was *Goal to Go*, which I read many times."
- Coach's words of wisdom: "The one thing I would advise young people is to enjoy whatever you are doing for the rest of your life— school, reading, working, playing, etc. If you enjoy what you are doing and this is a choice, you will do it so much better."
- "The most important thing I have learned is we will always have problems and difficulties. Life is a matter of choices. If you do drugs, drop out of school and run with bad people, you are probably choosing to go to jail. The one thing that will determine your success or failure are the choices you make. Follow these three rules and you will enjoy success and happiness:

1. Do right.
2. Do your best.
3. Show people you care.

You violate these three rules, you are choosing to have a life of problems. It is not complicated. Choose to follow these three rules."

Goal to Go is a 1931 book by Harold M. Sherman (1898–1987). It's about two pals, Tubby and Shrimp, who play on their college football and baseball teams. At first no one takes Shrimp seriously because he's so small, but Tubby stands up for him. Making things tough for Shrimp is that his brother is a great athlete for a rival school.

13

TOM KURVERS, HOCKEY

The World Traveler

Some people spend vacations traveling across the country or around the world. Others wait 'til they retire to see the sights. Tom Kurvers did it the only way he knew how: Playing hockey.

If you added all the miles between the places where Tom played professional hockey, it would equal 15,000! And that doesn't even count the traveling he did for 12 professional seasons, playing nearly 500 games on the road.

Tom's journeys actually started in the Twin Cities, named for Minneapolis and the capital of Minnesota, St. Paul. The Twin Cities are nestled in the southeastern part of the state right on the Wisconsin border. Minnesota—known as the "Land of 10,000 Lakes"—is a diverse state, with everything from mining in the far north near Canada to farming. But the one constant Minnesotans enjoy is hockey.

Like many kids in the Twin Cities, Tom grew up with hockey all around him. The Minnesota North Stars of the National Hockey League (NHL) played nearby, and the University of Minnesota always had a strong team. In fact, Tom's family had season tickets to see the Golden Gophers at the university. When Tom was growing up, he put up a net in his garage and practiced for hours slamming puck after puck, trying to perfect his shot. A defenseman, he fought through injuries—he had a broken thumb and a hurt leg—to lead the Bloomington Jefferson High School Jaguars to their first state tournament run his senior year.

For Minnesota, high school hockey is like basketball in central Indiana or football in Texas. It captures fans' hearts, and tournament games often are shown on television and played before thousands of people. Tom learned quickly, though, that it takes more than just a bunch of talented guys on the ice to win games. His high school coach, Tom Saterdalen, called him a "great role model."[1] In addition to being an honor student off the ice, Tom was the team leader. Right after he was named captain, he approached the coaches and said he would keep the players focused and out of trouble. His leadership worked. Years later, Coach Saterdalen said, "He kept his word, and we never had a closer group of players."[2] That camaraderie Tom fostered on the team, along with hard work in the rink, led the Jaguars to a 20–1–2 record going into the state tournament. Camaraderie—good will among friends or teammates—is important for players. The team skated to a third-place finish before 19,000 fans. More than 25 years later, Tom was named to his high school team's hall of fame, and a publication ranked Tom as the 54th greatest high school player ever to come out of Minnesota.

When it came time for college, though, not too many schools were interested. Tom was a good player, but he was still improving. He hadn't hit his peak. He was hoping the University of Minnesota would offer him a scholarship, but it never happened. Another hockey powerhouse, the University of Wisconsin, wanted him to play for its team but offered only a partial scholarship.

"I didn't have a choice as much as some guys," Tom once said. "Like most kids from the Twin Cities, I was pretty disappointed when the hometown team didn't recruit me as hard as some other players, but that's the way it is."[3]

But one school saw something in Tom. The University of Minnesota–Duluth, about 150 miles to the north, liked Tom's playing. He was considered a "defenseman with an offensive flair." That meant even though he often was in position on the ice to protect the puck and prevent the other team from scoring, he did a pretty good job scoring goals, too. He was especially dangerous from the "point," the area where the blue line meets the boards.

Duluth was close enough for Tom's family to see him play often. The school played in the Western Collegiate Hockey Association (WCHA), the best conference for college hockey. Like high school, Tom became captain of his team. And like high school, Tom had a great career. It was capped off by two amazing events on two consecutive days. First, on a brisk Friday afternoon in Lake Placid, New York, scores of fans who had gathered for the college hockey championship heard an official announcement: Tom Kurvers had won the Hobey Baker Award.

Hobey Baker had been a great player at Princeton University many years ago. He became the first US-born player inducted into the Hockey Hall of Fame. At 5 foot 9 and 160 pounds, Baker wasn't a big man, but it didn't matter. "Hobey had astonishing speed on the ice and the grace of a figure skater," wrote sportswriter Ron Fimrite.[4] Since 1981, the award has been given to the nation's best college hockey player. It is that sport's equivalent of the Heisman Trophy, which goes to the best college football player each year. Tom's family and coach, Mike Sertich, looked on as the announcement was made. Everyone was proud of the likeable young defenseman, who was the school's first Hobey Baker Award winner.

Coach Sertich said after the ceremony, "I couldn't be more proud of him. I hope my kids grow up to be like him."[5]

But the excitement didn't end for Tom and his Duluth Bulldog teammates. The next day, Bowling Green State University and Minnesota–Duluth met in the championship game. No one would ever forget it.

College basketball has the Final Four, and college hockey has the Frozen Four. A sellout crowd filled the arena as the teams faced off. At least six players on both teams that day eventually would go on to play professionally. Bowling Green was ranked fourth in the nation, but Duluth was ranked first. And the Duluth players had the memory of a former coach named Ralph Romano on their minds. Ralph had died while watching the team play in December, and the Bulldogs wore a patch with his initials to remember their friend.

The teams battled to a tie, then went to several overtimes and, finally, sudden death. That's when a game is played to break a tie, with the winning team being the first one to score. The outcome is determined by the score and not the clock. When it was over, Bowling Green came out on top, 5–4. It was the longest men's college hockey championship game ever. The game officially took 97 minutes, 11 seconds to play over almost four hours! The Duluth goalie was a freshman named Rick Kosti, who made 55 saves in the game.

"The championship game itself was amazing. I don't think college hockey had seen a game like that before," Coach Sertich said.[6]

Years later, when Tom would run into a player from that Bowling Green team, they would talk about the game. "The comforting thing is . . . they don't hold it over our heads. They consider it, like all hockey players when you're done playing, it's like you all played on the same team. We know we played in a pretty big-time game."[7]

Losing the game wasn't the only disappointment Tom felt in 1984. He had tried out for the US Olympic team, but he didn't make it. He didn't let it get him down, however.

"When he did not make the Olympic team in 1984 he felt bad," said Coach Saterdalen, his high school coach. "We talked for about an hour. When we finished talking, he left me by saying 'they made a mistake by not picking me.'" His coach remembered Tom saying he would "show them I'm going to be the best player in college hockey."[8] With the Hobey Baker Award, he was just that.

Coach Sertich knew what Tom had done and that not making the Olympic team had motivated his former star. "Tom took that experience . . . and turned it into something positive," he said.[9]

Even though his team lost in that championship game, Tom would remember his college career fondly. "There's something about college hockey—the skill, the talent, the daring—where you go as hard as you can, and that's what I remember."[10]

Tom's college career was ending, but his professional one was just beginning. The famed Montreal Canadiens had drafted Tom. The Canadiens were an old, established NHL team—one of the "original six," as they are known. The term refers to the four American and two Canadian teams that made up the NHL when the league was starting out. They are the Boston Bruins, Chicago Blackhawks, Detroit Red Wings, Montreal Canadiens, New York Rangers, and Toronto Maple Leafs.

In Tom they got a player who was dangerous on the power play and considered classy off the ice, too. His teammates called him "Kurvball."[11] Montreal—with their famed blue, red and white uniforms—used to be known for having the best French-Canadian players on its team. But when Tom started playing with them things changed. For the first time, the Canadiens had as many Americans on their roster as French-Canadians.

Although hockey is a tough game that demands a lot of hard work to become great, players know how to have fun. For instance, the rookies on the team had to go through an initiation from the veterans, who had the players sit for a special haircut—they had their heads shaved. The rookie initiation kept the team loose.

Tom spent the first three years of his professional career in Montreal. Trades are, of course, part of most professional sports, and Tom was not immune to them. He ended up playing for seven NHL teams. Once he landed in Anaheim, California, to play for the Mighty Ducks. He was met at the airport by a team official. The official spotted Tom's luggage: A duffel bag with a New York Islanders logo, another bag with a New Jersey Devils emblem, and yet another one with a Buffalo Sabres symbol—all teams Tom had played with. It was all part of the game.

Another time, while he was with the New Jersey Devils, Tom was involved in a game that would be remembered not for what players did on the ice but for what his coach *said*. In 1988, New Jersey was playing the Boston Bruins in the playoffs. Coach Jim Schoenfeld was frustrated at a referee named Don Koharski. After the game on the way to the locker room, Coach Schoenfeld yelled at the referee, "You fat pig! Have another doughnut! Have another doughnut!" The incident was caught on tape and has been replayed many times. (The coach and referee have since made up.)

Tom finished his playing career by competing in Seibu, Japan, near Tokyo. Japanese referees in Japan called a tighter game than in the United States, so they were wary of rough play. Tom had a fun time in his year there with the Seibu Bears and learning a little about the culture. Around the time he was playing, a Hollywood movie called *Mr. Baseball* came out. Tom Selleck starred as an American baseball player who goes to Japan to play. So Tom's Japanese teammates started calling him "Mr. Baseball."[12]

Tom retired in 1996, but he never left the game. He spent time in the front office of the Phoenix Coyotes, working as director of player personnel alongside one of the greatest players ever, Wayne Gretzky. Tom also was a scout, watching hundreds of games in a year. He eventually moved on to Tampa, where he became assistant general manager. For the first time in his life, Tom had a desk job. Coordinating expenses, signing off on team affairs, and dealing with the league office on a variety of issues were just a few of the things Tom dealt with.

In late 2018, Tom developed a cough. He started feeling a little pain in his chest and thought he might be having a heart problem. Doctors examined him and at first didn't find anything wrong. But as time went by he didn't feel better and he went back to the doctor. Tom was shocked when he heard that he had lung cancer. That was a surprise because Tom didn't smoke and kept in good shape. But lung cancer can strike nonsmokers, and that's what happened to Tom.

He began taking a special drug to fight the cancer and had to stop traveling so much. So the guy who played all over and then kept traveling in his various roles with teams as a scout or front-office executive finally had to slow down.

"I'm going to fight," Tom told a reporter. "I'm living with cancer now."[13]

In one way Tom Kurvers' journeys sent him thousands of miles from arena to arena. But in another, he really was settled down the whole time, at home in the sport he loves, hockey.

Tom says:

- Tom's favorite books: "Sports biographies and newspaper reports of sports-related content."
- Tom's words of wisdom: "Pursue what interests *you* the most, and generally that is what you are most likely good at in the first place."
- Tom's obstacles: "Being cut from a team or rejected from an activity is just a re-direction in your pursuit. Keep doing what you like to do, work hard, and know your perseverance will be rewarded."

14

VERNON LAW, BASEBALL

The Deacon on the Mound

As a boy in the 1930s and 1940s, Vernon Law probably never dreamed his life's path would take him from the peaceful surroundings of small-town life in Idaho to the soot-filled streets of Pittsburgh.

All it would take was a lot of talent and the help of one of the most famous singers ever.

The Laws were a large family, living in Meridian, Idaho, with an outhouse in the back and a dirt basement. Vern and his brother, Evan, were close in age and were best pals. They played football and baseball together.

One day a man named Herman Welker was watching Vern pitch in high school. Vern was doing well, and Herman, a local lawyer, was impressed. Herman had some important connections. He used to work in Hollywood, and he was friends with a famous singer named Bing Crosby. Bing was a singer who is known for "White Christmas," among other hit songs, and he acted in many movies and loved golf. Herman and Bing used to go hunting together in Idaho. It so happened that Bing had become part owner of the Pittsburgh Pirates.

Word soon got out that Vernon Law was a good pitcher. But what many folks didn't know was how religious he was. Vern and his family were members of the Church of Jesus Christ of Latter-day Saints, some-times known as LDS, or Mormons. In fact, even at a young age, Vern had become a deacon and could teach in the church. Compared to many

religions, Mormonism is somewhat new; it was started in the United States less than 200 years ago. Mormonism forbids the use of alcohol and tobacco.

Herman and Bing knew this about Vernon, and they also knew scouts from other teams were going to try to sign the young pitcher. So they hatched a plan. And it came at a busy time for Vernon. He got engaged to his sweetheart, VaNita, the same day he graduated from high school. The very next day, nine men—all scouts from Major League teams—showed up at the Law house. Eight of them were smoking cigars. Vernon's father told them if they kept the cigars out, they could come in. One at a time they made their pitches about how Vernon would be great, how much their clubs needed him, and how much money he would make. Vernon's father and mother listened. Finally, the last scout came in. He was not smoking a cigar. Instead, he had brought a dozen roses and a box of chocolates. All of a sudden, the Laws' phone rang. In small-town Idaho in the 1940s, the family didn't receive many calls. Vernon's mother answered. Who was on the other line but Bing Crosby—the famous singer who Mrs. Law loved! And guess who Vernon signed with?

The best part of the story, though, was the sneaky plan. You see, Bing knew that the Laws didn't like smoking, but the other scouts there didn't. So he told the Pirate scout to buy cigars for the other fellows.

After a short stint in the minors, Vernon and VaNita headed to Pittsburgh to start their new life. The only problem was the Pirates were horrible. They were known by the baseball expression "cellar-dwellers." Starting with 1950, Vernon's first year with the team, the Pirates finished last or second-to-last every season for eight years. That isn't fun for the players, or the fans.

But Vernon was shaping up to be a dependable teammate. He had good control and didn't serve up too many walks. Third-baseman Don Hoak described him as "a quiet guy but tough."[1] Teammate Wally Westlake nicknamed him "the deacon" because of his ties to his church.[2] Vernon also was known to have a good memory, which is important for pitchers who need to remember what type of pitch a hitter likes—or doesn't. And he was durable. In one game in July 1955 at Pittsburgh's Forbes Field, Vernon's manager asked him to pitch because the scheduled starter was hurt. Vernon didn't complain, he just walked out to the mound. At the end of nine innings, the game was tied. The game wore on in the summer heat. Vernon stayed in. In the 15th inning, his manager tried to take him out but Vernon pleaded as best he could to stay in. "Skip," he said, "let me win or lose this darn thing!"[3] So he continued on, until he was taken out after 18 innings. That's the equivalent of throwing two games! Another pitcher came in and, wouldn't you know it, won the game in the 19th. In all, Vernon pitched for almost five hours that day. (Amazingly, he pitched only four days later, winning a 13-inning game.)

Vernon remains the last Major League pitcher to throw 18 innings in a game.

That's a record that probably will not be broken. In those days baseball was a little different. Teams had four starting pitchers, not five like today. And starting pitchers were expected to finish what they started. There weren't many relief pitchers back then.

On the field, Vernon developed into a fine player. Pitchers sometimes throw at batters to get them to move off the plate. Not Vernon. He had been hit once, so he knew how much it hurt, and he did not want to run the risk of seriously injuring another player. Off the field, while many of his teammates would stay out late, Vernon preferred to divide his time between his family and speaking to various groups. He donated a lot of time to a local children's hospital.

Vernon also had a hobby. He compiled short sayings—some of his own, some from other people he quoted. The spiral red notebook would stay with him for years. He called the book "Words to Live By."[4] He jotted rules about being on the field, like "I will never insist I am right to the extent of angering others." He also wrote "Difficulty can be the means of opening up a new opportunity."[5]

When 1960 rolled around, the Pirates started to do something consistently they hadn't done in a long time: They started winning. Often, they made things exciting by coming from behind in late innings. They had a great outfielder from Puerto Rico named Roberto Clemente, who would wind up in the Hall of Fame. They had Elroy Face, one of the game's first relief specialists. Shortstop Dick Groat was the team's captain. A second baseman named Bill Mazeroski would become famous by the end of the season. And of course they had Vernon Law, who by this point had been with the Pirates longer than any of his teammates.

"We had a lot of different personalities" on the 1960 team, Vernon once said.[6] In fact, some of the rowdier ones ended up causing a big problem for Vernon as the season wound down. The night the Pirates clinched the pennant, the players showered, dressed in their street clothes, and piled into the team bus, whooping and hollering. They were going to the World Series to face the mighty New York Yankees. Guys started horsing around, cutting off each other's ties. When they got on the bus, they saw Vernon sitting there and decided it would be fun to take off his shoes. But when they piled on, someone yanked Vernon's right foot too hard, and he cried out. Immediately, the players quieted and let their star pitcher be. Vernon's ankle stated throbbing, and it was an injury that he—and the team—could not afford. He was going to be their starter in Game 1 of the World Series—and what a series it was to be.

Vernon wasn't going to let his team down, and he never blamed anyone for the accident. But because he favored his leg, he altered his pitching motion. This started giving him shoulder problems. He could do nothing but try to ignore it.

Vernon was one of the few Pirates who had played in Yankee Stadium before. Earlier that year, he pitched in the classic old park, winning one of that year's two All-Star games. He went into Game 1 with the confidence of his manager, Danny Murtaugh, and was "unruffled," as one writer put it, against the powerful Yankees. Coincidentally, the last time the Pirates were in a World Series had been in 1927, against one of the greatest teams ever—the Yankees, who were known as "Murderers' Row" because of their strong lineup. In 1960, Vern had the best year of his career. But when he walked to the mound in Game 1 in Forbes Field, he was limping. He remained confident, though. The Yankees managed to scatter 10 hits, but the Pirate bats came to life. Vernon earned the victory as Pittsburgh won Game 1, 6–4.

But the Yankees wouldn't stay down for long. They clobbered the Pirates 16–3 and 10–0 in the next two games. Their great star, Mickey Mantle, had six hits, seven runs batted in (RBIs), and three home runs. Manager Murtaugh named Vernon his Game 4 starter, and the Deacon didn't disappoint. Before 67,000 fans in the stadium known as "the house that Ruth built"—a tribute to the former great Yankee slugger Babe Ruth—Vernon pitched a solid game, striking out five hitters in the 3–2 win. He even had two hits himself and scored a run. His fifth-inning double was a key factor in helping the Pirates. (One of the game's first great stars, "The Babe" played most of his 22-year career with the Yankees. He was known for his large appetite and ability to hit home runs.)

The interesting thing is that years earlier, Vernon had to do some soul-searching about whether he would ever play on Sundays, a day for prayer in his faith. But he also felt an obligation to his team. In the end, he decided to play, which was a good thing for Pirate fans in the 1960 World Series, because Game 4 fell on a Sunday.

Vernon always stayed true to the guidelines set forth by his religion. Before Game 6, Vernon received a call from a cigarette company, wanting to know if he wanted to endorse their product. Vernon said thanks, but no thanks. "I told them I wasn't going to compromise my principles and faith," he said.[7]

Maybe the call was a bad omen for the Pirates, because the Yankees won 12–0. The teams headed to a decisive and final Game 7.

"I knew if I did a good job, we'd win," he said in John Moody's biography, *Kiss It Good-Bye.* "It was that simple."[8] The game would be remembered for many things. At one point, trainers rushed onto the field after Yankee shortstop Tony Kubek took a hard hop in the throat, knocking him down for a few minutes. The scoring was back and forth, exciting the almost 37,000 fans who had turned out in the steel town with hope in their hearts. Again, manager Murtaugh called on his ace, who hobbled his way to the mound. The Pirates gave Vernon a quick lead, scoring two in the first and two more in the second. Vernon pitched into the sixth inning, then was pulled for a reliever. He had given his all, winning two of the series games. Now it was up to the bullpen.

The Yankees didn't quit as they took a 5–4 lead. The Pirates then exploded for five runs in the eighth. By the time Pittsburgh came to bat in the ninth, the score was tied, 9–9.

Yankees pitcher Ralph Terry dug in against Pirate Bill Mazeroski. The 24-year-old second baseman took the first pitch for ball one. Terry wheeled back and fired the next pitch, and Mazeroski cracked it deep into left field. Outfielder Yogi Berra raced back to the fence, but it didn't matter. The Pirates had won the World Series, four games to three.

To this day, fans remember the game as one of the greatest World Series contests ever. Mickey Mantle, a hero to many Yankee fans over the years, said it was the low point of his career. Not so for Mazeroski, whose "walk-off" home run is considered one of the most dramatic ever. At least one writer said Vernon was "the difference" in the series.

As years went by, teammates remembered Vernon with kind words.

"I'm a better person for having known Vern," said fellow pitcher Bob Friend.[9]

"There were people I admired, Vernon for one. He was open to all personalities and always kind," said George Witt.[10]

And Mazeroski, the hero of Game 7, said, "Vernon Law was a special person. If you couldn't look up to Vernon Law, you can't look up to anyone. I have as much respect for him as I do for anyone."[11]

Vernon continued playing for the Pirates, but the shoulder problems he encountered continued to nag him. In 1965, he went 17–9 and won the comeback player of the year award. When Vernon retired in 1967, a Pittsburgh sportswriter named Charley Feeney wrote, "Law, a class guy, will be missed."[12]

Vernon never really left baseball, though. He eventually became the coach at Brigham Young University in Salt Lake City, an area of the country where many Mormons reside. Salt Lake City is the capital of Utah and the state's largest city. Later, after his son Vance became coach, Vernon stayed to help out and became a big supporter of the university sports teams. Even as an older man, he used to throw batting practice, saying he could "still throw hard enough to make it challenging for kids."[13] Before road trips, he would bring chocolate milk and doughnuts to both the baseball and women's basketball teams.

Vance always remained proud of his father. "He was the first famous member of the church that was a professional athlete," said Vance, who was himself a big-leaguer from 1980 to 1991.[14]

For his part, Vernon remains a satisfied man. "I wouldn't trade my life with anybody else. I played during the golden day of baseball, back when it was a game and when it was fun."[15]

Vernon says:

- Vern's favorite books: "There were a couple of books that I enjoyed growing up. They were *Huckleberry Finn* and *Tom Sawyer*. The reason was I enjoyed a bit of adventure myself, and I was imagining I could do those same kinds of things."
- Vern's words of wisdom: "The advice I'd give to kids is to be teachable. Listen to your mom and dad, teachers and coaches as they have the experience and can really help you reach your goals."
- "There is a story about a coach wanting this good baseball player to play centerfield, but the boy told the coach, 'I'm a shortstop, and if I can't play shortstop I'm going to take my glove and go home.' The coach explained to the boy 'With your speed you could really help our team,' but the boy refused and went home. This boy was not teachable, but only thinking of himself, was also very selfish, and not a team player. My son Vance became a big-league player and an All-Star because he could play all infield positions, because he was teachable at every position. You had to develop different skills."

- "So the best thing I learned was from coaches that had experience and taught me how to take a proper wind-up, how to throw a changeup, and how to get good hitters out by changing speeds, etc."
- Vern's obstacles: "I had very few obstacles to overcome, but a couple of big ones: I tore my rotator cuff in my shoulder twice, and it really took a lot of hard work and patience to work through the pain that kept me from being successful, but I was able to do that and had my best year in 1965."

Samuel Clemens (1835–1910), better known as Mark Twain, wrote The Adventures of Tom Sawyer, *which was published in 1876, and* The Adventures of Huckleberry Finn, *which was published in 1884. They take place in a fictional town in Missouri. Tom is an orphan who lives with his aunt. Huck has a father who has troubles of his own, so he is left on his own to independently entertain himself. He and Tom are pals.*

15

KRISTINE LILLY, SOCCER

The Caps Queen

The teams had battled all day. Exhausted but desperate to score, China and the United States had competed under a hot July sun in the 1999 Women's World Cup soccer championship. China attacked. Sun Wen kicked the ball, and it went out of bounds off a US defender. This meant a corner kick for the Chinese. It was sudden death, the 100th minute of play in the 0–0 game. Liu Ying carefully took the kick, bending it toward the goal, where her teammate Fan Yunjie headed the ball past US goalkeeper Briana Scurry. Then, all of a sudden, a white jersey with No. 13 came out of nowhere. The player leaped and headed the ball back out—no goal!

That white jersey belonged to Kristine Lilly, a 5 foot 4 midfielder for the Americans. Sudden death ended, and now the coaches each sent five players for penalty kicks. One by one, with a remarkable 90,185 fans watching, they took their turns. China kicked first, and scored. Then Carla Overbeck scored for the United States. China's second kick was good, and again the US team tied it, with a shot from Joy Fawcett. Then Scurry saved the next Chinese shot. The crowd in Pasadena, California, cheered. Kristine then stepped up and calmly hit her shot to the left side, close to the spot where moments before she had saved the game with her header. China made their next kick. US star Mia Hamm approached the ball, made her shot, and then slapped hands with Kristine. China made another. It was down to one final kick. Brandi Chastain raced to the ball

and kicked as the Chinese goalie dove to her left. It sailed between the goalie and the post of the net. The United States had won the World Cup!

It was, as a writer for the *New York Daily News*, Wayne Coffey, wrote after the game, "the greatest day women's soccer has ever had in this country."[1] Forty million Americans watched on television. If people didn't know anything about the US players before the game, they did now. They were sought after for autographs and interviews, and parades across the country celebrated their achievement.

The US team was ecstatic about the win, but took Kristine's play in stride. "She was doing her job—nothing more, nothing less," said Brandi Chastain.[2]

Scurry said she didn't even realize Kristine was behind her. Long before the game, Coach Tony DiCicco had said, "There's no replacement for Kristine. She's very versatile. She can play a lot of places, and she just makes the game happen wherever she is."[3]

"I had no time to think, no time to react," Kristine said later.[4]

For Kristine, it was a great moment in a great career.

Kristine grew up in Wilton, Connecticut. She started playing soccer at age six. The sport's attraction to her then was as much about the orange slices at halftime as anything else, she once told a reporter. Then, there weren't many girls' soccer teams around. From ages 8 to 14 she played on a boys team. She became better playing for the Wilton Wonders and then moved on to high school, where people would really take notice of her game. Kristine's high school team played in four consecutive state title games, and in the next four years, her college, the University of North Carolina, also played in four straight national championships. In that eight-year span, her teams won seven times! In 1991, she was awarded the Hermann Trophy, given to the nation's best men's and women's college soccer players.

Even before college, Kristine was asked to join the US national team. This is a great honor, being able to play all over the world. The two big stages are the World Cup and the Olympics, where teams representing their countries compete every four years. Kristine played in five World Cups and three Olympics. She played so well for so long that she holds an amazing distinction: She is the youngest player and the oldest player to score for the US team. Kristine also is known for her "caps." When soccer players compete in international play, they receive a cap. Many years ago players received actual hats that were kind of like badges, but that stopped over time. Kristine earned 354 caps in her career, which is the most by any soccer player ever.

Her brother Scott once said his sister reminds him of a duck. A duck looks calm on the surface, but underneath her feet paddle furiously.

Kristine played in many memorable games with great teammates. She was part of the 1996 team in Atlanta that won Olympic gold for the first time. She also found time to play for a team in Sweden and even became one of the few women to compete in a men's indoor league in Washington. She also was captain for a women's team called the Boston Breakers.

Even though Kristine and her teammates traveled across the globe, they found time to enjoy themselves. They played board games like Trivial Pursuit and Scrabble and watched movies together. Doing things like that gives everyone a spirit of camaraderie. And because she played for so long, sometimes the other players teased her, calling her "Grandma."[5]

But players can't play forever, not even Kristine. She announced her retirement in early 2011 and now has time to spend with her family. Since she grew up so close to New York, Kristine cheers for the New York Jets in football, the Yankees in baseball, and the Knicks in basketball. Off the field, she keeps in shape. She took pride in being known for her exceptional conditioning during her playing days. In 2012, she trained to run in the Boston Marathon, a 26.2-mile race. Boston's race is world famous and takes place every April. And she continues to be a role model for girls.

"I'm always optimistic. It's important for girls who have dreams to have a place to play, and for communities to see women's sports out there."[6]

But she hasn't left soccer. She runs Kristine Lilly Soccer Academy and, in 2012, was named an assistant coach of the Breakers.

Kristine's accomplishments are remembered fondly by many in the soccer world.

Sunil Gulati, a former president for US Soccer, said this about Kristine:

> Kristine Lilly has been an integral part of our women's soccer history, a great ambassador for the game and a tremendous role model. Her accomplishments speak for themselves, but her lasting legacy will be one of a player totally dedicated to the team and doing whatever it took on and off the field to produce success.[7]

When she ended her playing career, she summed up her days competing on soccer fields this way: "I did whatever I could, I did the best I could," she said. "I feel good about that."[8]

Kristine says:

- Kristine's favorite books: "I loved to read as a kid and I still do. I loved reading the Dr. Seuss books, and I read them now to my little girl. Some other books that stand out for me were: *The Giving Tree, Charlotte's Web, The Call of the Wild, Tales of a Fourth Grade Nothing*, and *How to Eat Fried Worms*. I love animals, and the *Call of the Wild* was about wolves. *The Giving Tree* just showed how we should be to others, and the tree just kept giving and never asked for anything in return. I just loved *Charlotte's Web* and the same with *Tales of a Fourth Grade Nothing* and *How to Eat Fried Worms*. I just remembered them so I must have liked them."

- Kristine's words of wisdom: "My advice to young kids is to work hard and surround yourself with people who want to help you! Have fun with whatever you do. I didn't really have many obstacles when I was young. It wasn't so popular for girls to play sports so I just kept playing even though it was a little different for girls to play."
- Kristine's inspiration: "My brother was my role model growing up!"

E. B. White (1899–1985) wrote Charlotte's Web, *which came out in 1952 and is about the friendship between a pig named Wilbur and a spider named Charlotte. Jack London (1876–1916) wrote* The Call of the Wild, *which came out in 1903. This adventure book is about a dog named Buck who becomes a sled dog in Canada.* Tales of a Fourth Grade Nothing, *by Judy Blume (1938–), is about nine-year-old Peter and his annoying little brother, Fudge. Thomas Rockwell (1933–) wrote* How to Eat Fried Worms, *which came out in 1973. It is about a boy named Billy who is bet he cannot eat a worm for 15 days.*

16

KIM MULKEY, BASKETBALL

Champion Player, Champion Coach

At first, Kim Mulkey might not have looked like a dominating basketball player. Only 5 foot 4, her pigtails hanging behind her, she could be the smallest person on the court, but give her the ball and watch her go.

Kim grew up in Tickfaw, Louisiana, a town about 60 miles north of New Orleans. The two things she loved most growing up in the 1970s were her family and competition. At age 12, she entered a roller-skating marathon and almost won, skating against many folks older than her for 23 hours, 55 minutes. She played baseball on a boys team and did well enough to become an all-star. Her dad played one-on-one basketball with her, and she just kept getting better. School was no different. She wanted to do well, so she sat in the front row to learn as much as she possibly could. Those habits—working hard in school or on the court—carried into high school.

"I was a little adult. I wasn't into slumber parties," she once said. "I was happy, but happy was sitting with my grandmother on a porch swing with a Barq's root beer."[1]

She led her Hammond High School team to four state titles. Once, she scored 60 points in one game. She graduated with a 4.0 grade-point average and was named valedictorian. She even had perfect attendance through all of high school. Kim likes to tell the funny story of being late for the awards ceremony honoring her for her attendance because she was coming back from a recruiting trip!

If you were to keep a checklist of Kim's achievements in basketball, you can start here. Because if Kim Mulkey is playing for a team or coaching one, you can bet they are going to become a champion. High school? Check. Now on to college. Several schools were interested in Kim, and many people expected her to head west down the road to the state capital, Baton Rouge, to attended Louisiana State University. Louisiana's state capital of more than 200,000 people sits about 70 miles northwest of New Orleans. The Mississippi River runs along its western border.

But she opted for Louisiana Tech, a smaller school just south of Arkansas. Fans there didn't know it, but Kim was about to stay for a long time.

Louisiana Tech had its share of great athletes over the years, from Terry Bradshaw in football to Karl Malone in basketball. But few had as much success at the school as Kim, who one writer called a "magician" because of her ball-handling skills.[2] She also was described as a "sparkplug" and "a tiny fireball."[3] Fans even started braiding their hair the way Kim did her pigtails. With Kim playing guard on a talented team, the Lady Techsters recorded 54 consecutive wins, four Final Four appearances and two national championships. Success as a college player? Check.

Kim was living and breathing basketball. When she wasn't playing for Louisiana Tech, she was on the court for the US team. It was a chance to travel the world. In 1984, that team won the gold medal in the Olympics, which were held that year in Los Angeles. Another team, another title. Check.

Kim was the first person in her family to graduate from college. Tickfaw held a parade in her honor, and the town came out to celebrate Kim, who wore her gold medal.

So now what? Professional basketball for women was in its infancy. Kim thought about going to business school to continue her education. But Sonja Hogg and Leon Barmore, her coaches at Louisiana Tech, had other ideas. They asked her: How would you like to be an assistant coach? So Kim entered the next phase of her career: Coaching. Her first order of business was recruiting. That's a big part of what college coaches do, traveling all over the country looking for the best high school players and deciding who will be offered scholarships.

She and Coach Barmore traveled all over, trying to find the best players possible to compete at Louisiana Tech. During games, Coach Mulkey had many duties, not the least of which was being Coach Barmore's "coattail holder," as one sportswriter put it.[4] If Coach Barmore became excited and tried to run onto the court, it was Coach Mulkey's job to tug him back. She ended up spending 15 years at her alma mater as an assistant. A highlight came in 1988, when the Lady Techsters edged Auburn by two points to win the national title. Success as an assistant coach who worked hard to prepare for opponents and recruit players? Another check.

Then the day came for Coach Barmore to retire. Everyone expected Coach Mulkey to be the perfect person to take over the program. But it didn't happen. Louisiana Tech officials and Coach Mulkey could not agree on a contract. For fans 300 miles to the west, in Waco, Texas, that was a good thing. That's because Baylor University, a school with about 15,000 students, immediately signed Kim to be their coach.

Right away, she started whipping the Lady Bears into shape. And it didn't take long. In her first year, 2000–2001, Baylor did something it had never done before: It made the NCAA Women's Basketball Tournament. Coach Mulkey was rewarded with a contract extension as she settled in to the Big 12 school. She worked hard, guiding the team in practice and recruiting all over. She also tried to find ways to relax, like gardening and listening to gospel or country music, but basketball was always a primary concern for Coach Mulkey. And that concern now was making Baylor a contender. Baylor did nothing but improve under her leadership. She put a "thought for the day" on a board before each practice to remind them what they need to accomplish. One time, five of her players were interviewed and asked to describe their coach in one word. Four used the same word: "Intense."[5]

"I tell my kids up front that I coach off of emotion," she said.[6] That emotion motivated her players just fine. The Lady Bears won their first national title in 2005.

As a player, Coach Mulkey had won a state title in high school and a national championship in college, and the Olympic gold medal. As an assistant coach, she won a national title. Now she was the head coach of the champion Lady Bears. Things couldn't get better, could they?

They did.

A few years later, Coach Mulkey recruited a young woman named Brittney Griner. Coaches all over the country wanted Brittney to play for their college. At 6 foot 8, she was what is known as a "game-changer." She influenced the sport the way her new coach, Kim, had done years earlier. She chose Baylor and had an immediate impact.

In 2011, the Lady Bears looked great—unstoppable, some would say. They raced through the regular season and made the NCAA Women's Basketball Tournament as the number-one seed. It seemed liked everyone was picking them to win the championship. To do that meant Baylor would have to do something no school had done—win 40 games.

They started the tournament against the University of California, Santa Barbara, running over the Gauchos in an easy win. Brittney played only 22 minutes but made most of her shots in the 81–40 win. Next up were the Florida Gators. Coach Mulkey, often crouching on the sidelines and yelling instructions to her players, watched intently as both teams shot long-range baskets. In the end, Baylor came out on top, 76–57. Something happened in that game that people will remember for a long time: Brittney Griner became the second player *ever* to dunk in an NCAA Women's Basketball Tournament game. Something else happened, too, that many fans might have missed. In the postgame handshake, Coach Mulkey pulled a Florida player aside to offer special words of encouragement. Good sportsmanship is also part of coaching.

Georgia Tech came next for Baylor, and Brittney was ready for the challenge. She scored 35 points. On one play, teammate Brooklyn Pope passed her the ball, and Brittney leaped high to slam a thundering dunk. It was an exclamation on the game, which Baylor won, 83–68.

The next challenge for Baylor was Tennessee. Coached by the legendary Pat Summitt, the Volunteers were always tough. But Baylor would not be denied. "Defense wins ballgames for you," Coach Mulkey said after the game, and she was right. The Lady Bears won, 77–58.[7]

The Final Four waited for Baylor, who had to face Stanford. Before the game it was announced that Brittney was named player of the year, and Coach Mulkey was honored as coach of the year. Now, if the Lady Bears could hang on for two more games, they would be national champs. Like many teams, Stanford had to worry about defending Brittney. But it was two of her teammates who provided the spark for the Lady Bears. Destiny Williams had 10 rebounds and Terran Condrey scored 13 points, leading Baylor to a 59–47 victory. It proved a point Coach Mulkey made when she said, "This team is more than Brittney Griner."[8]

Now 39–0, the Lady Bears faced a tough Notre Dame team. The two were closely matched, and the game remained tight. The Irish crept to within three points, but that was as close as they got. When the final horn sounded, Brittney Griner had 26 points, 13 rebounds, and five blocks. Baylor was the national champion for the second time under Coach Mulkey, who hugged each and every one of her players, thanking them. They had worked together and became the first NCAA women's basketball team to win 40 games.

In 2007, Coach Mulkey cowrote a book about her life called *Won't Back Down: Teams, Dreams, and Family*. She probably wished she had waited a few years to write about the great 2011–2012 team! When the team arrived back in Waco, about 2,000 fans greeted them—and their champion coach.

Baylor continued to have success with Coach Mulkey leading the way. They routinely won more than 30 games in a season.

In 2019, the Bears had another good season and made it to the championship game against Notre Dame. Lauren Cox, one of Baylor's star players, left the game with a knee injury. Notre Dame, which at one point was down 17 points, climbed back into the game.

But with 33 seconds remaining, Baylor's Chloe Jackson took a pass and raced to her right, leaped in the air, and launched a one-handed shot. It sailed through the net and gave the Lady Bears the lead. When the buzzer went off Baylor had won, 82–81, capturing its third national title under Coach Mulkey. And they won an amazing 29 consecutive games that season.

A year after Baylor won the national title, two great things happened in Coach Mulkey's life. First, in February 2020, Baylor beat Texas Tech, 77–62. The game was more than just another victory; it was Coach Mulkey's 600th win in 700 games. She had won 600 games faster than any basketball coach—male or female. Then, not long after, Coach Mulkey learned she was being inducted into the Naismith Basketball Memorial Hall of Fame in Springfield, Massachusetts.

So the champion player who became a champion coach is recognized officially as one of the best the sport has to offer.

As one writer put it years ago, "Kim Mulkey is accustomed to making history."[9]

Coach Mulkey says:

- Coach on reading: "Like most kids I did not read as much as I should have. In fact, the only books that I read were required reading for class. I did, however, enjoy articles in sports magazines, especially *Sports Illustrated*."
- Coach's words of wisdom: "The best thing I learned while trying to become successful is that I love to compete. Competing made me feel good! I competed in the classroom as well as in sports."

- Coach on obstacles: "Obstacles are a part of life. I have too many to name them all, but one obstacle that I remember was not being able to play on the All-Star team in baseball after being selected to the All-Star team. Because I was a girl, I was not allowed to play in the All-Star tournament that was held in another town."
- Coach's motivation: "My parents are responsible for helping me achieve all that I have achieved. They provided the support, the love, and the resources."
- "I am motivated each day because I am afraid to fail."

Soon after the 2020–21 season ended, Coach Mulkey surprised a lot of folks by announcing she would return to her home state to coach the Louisiana State University Tigers. Almost immediately, the school's ticket office started taking orders for the upcoming season. It looked to be a challenge—LSU was coming off a 9–13 season—but it was a chance for Coach Mulkey to do what she does best: Build a program, and win.

17

TY MURRAY, RODEO

The Record-Breaking Cowboy

Teachers often hear kids say they want to be a firefighter or astronaut when they grow up. When Ty Murray was young, he knew exactly what he wanted to do. Ty told his teacher he wanted to break Larry Mahan's record.

Larry was a rodeo champion who had won six All-Around Championship, and Ty said he wanted to be even better.

"I've known I wanted to be a professional cowboy since I was a little bitty kid."[1] It helped that he came from a long line of ranchers. He even came home from the hospital wearing tiny leather baby boots. His mother liked to say that his first words were that he wanted to be a bull rider. Ty used to ride his mother's sewing-machine case, pretending it was a bucking bull.

Ty and his family lived near Phoenix in the wintertime and in Albuquerque in the summer. Rodeo was in his blood. His dad competed in rodeos, and his mom was a former rodeo rider. When he was only nine years old, Ty got on a bull for the first time. "It was something that I was really serious about at a very young age and I never wavered from that," he said.[2]

While friends would go to football games, rodeo came first. Ty worked out with the high school gymnastics team to improve his balance for rodeo competition. Other kids often worked a job to save up to buy a

car, but Ty worked at a horse track one summer to raise money to buy a bucking machine so he could practice.

All that practice paid off. Ty became a good roughstock rider. In rodeo, roughstock is made up of three judged riding events—bareback, saddle bronc, and bull. The other events, like calf roping, are timed. Each event demands something different from a rider. Bareback requires riders to be strong and flexible. Saddle bronc is all about timing and balance. And bull riding—well, that's the really tough one. It's all about anticipating and reacting as you hang on, hoping for eight seconds not to get thrown from a 1,900-pound animal. Fans especially love bull riding. A cowboy is thrown from a bull once every 17 rides, making it extremely dangerous.

One day in the stands, Ty's mom heard a man say, "Who is that kid?"[3] She knew they were talking about her son. Another time Larry Mahan saw Ty ride, and the veteran rodeo man invited the young buck to his ranch to learn a few things. Ty was ecstatic, and he never forgot how generous Larry was with him.

Ty rode well enough to draw the interest of colleges offering rodeo scholarships, and he chose Odessa College in West Texas. Rodeo is the only college sport that allows competitors to be both amateur and professional. That meant Ty would compete for his school, but he was free to travel on his own time around the country and earn money in rodeos. Roughstock riders are awarded a dollar for each point earned; that's how standings are kept. The better the rides, the higher the point total.

Ty was fortunate to be surrounded by helpful people. On the road, he teamed with Cody Lambert, who was a few years older than Ty and who had a good sense of what it took to get from town to town. Ty knew rodeo, but when he started out he didn't have a clue about scheduling airline flights, renting cars, or mapping out his next trip. Cody took care of all that. Sometimes the two clashed; Ty was not a morning person, and Cody liked to yell at him to bounce out of bed in the morning. Ty did well in rodeos, and he kept his eye on an important title: All-Around Champion. That distinction goes to the cowboy who wins the most often while competing in at least two events. It's what Ty was gunning for, and that meant hanging on for rides on bucking animals with names like Sir Kickalot. Ty was so good at his events he was named Overall Rookie of the Year in the Professional Rodeo Cowboys Association.

The year 1989 would be bittersweet for Ty. At Wyoming's Cheyenne Frontier Days, one of the biggest rodeos each year, one of Ty's friends, Lane Frost, rode a bull named Taking Care of Business. He finished the ride, but after he landed on the dirt, the bull suddenly plowed into Lane, breaking several of the cowboy's ribs. The bull's force had hurt Lane badly, and he was immediately taken to a hospital. Doctors could not save him, and Lane died. Ty and his friends were shocked by what happened. It was the low point of the year for Ty. A few years later Hollywood came out with a movie called *8 Seconds* about Lane's life.

Ty had to stay focused because the National Finals Rodeo (NFR) was coming up, and he was going to be part of it. The NFR is 10 rounds of competition for the world's best riders, and it takes place in Las Vegas each December. And in 1989, Ty wanted more than anything to win. He hung on to his broncs and rode his bulls, and when the scores were tallied, Ty Murray sat atop the standings. The 20-year-old roughstock rider had become the All-Around Champion.

Being at the top of the standings became a habit for Ty. He would go on to win six consecutive All-Around titles. But the record he had told his teacher about all those years earlier—the seventh win—was what he wanted. No one had won seven All-Around Championships. But something suddenly derailed Ty's effort, something he rarely had to deal with before: injuries.

When he was still learning to ride, nine-year-old Ty had been thrown from a bull, who stepped on his face and broke his jaw. But he had been fortunate not to have had other serious injuries. About five months after his win in Las Vegas, Ty rode a saddle bronc named Road Agent at a rodeo in California. As he dismounted, Ty's left foot caught in the stirrup, and the next thing he knew he was on the ground, getting kicked by the horse. One of the kicks landed on Ty's right elbow, breaking it. Another time, a jittery horse reared and tossed Ty and then landed on the cowboy's right knee. Sometimes injuries come when you least expect them. Once, after a solid ride on a bull, Ty jumped off, but when he landed he felt something snap in his left knee. These and other injuries added up to Ty having to take some time off from the sport he loved, just as he was going for a record seventh title. And then a shoulder injury followed. It seemed liked every joint in Ty's 5 foot 8, 150-pound body was wrapped in a brace at one time or another.

The time off from rodeo made Ty appreciate his surroundings. He lived on a ranch in Texas, where he had time to enjoy wildlife. But Ty couldn't sit around. He needed to rehabilitate, and that takes a lot of work. Rehabilitation (often called "rehab" for short) is when athletes who have an injury must use therapy and exercise to restore a body part back to good health. He hired a trainer, who used special exercises to get Ty into "riding shape." It took a long time, and Ty was out of competition for several seasons, but he did it. He came back stronger than ever.

"I don't take my health for granted," he once wrote, "and nobody should."[4] When 1998 came around, Ty was ready. He competed as often as he could, spending as many as 250 days away from his beloved ranch. In the NFR, he and a cowboy named Herbert Theriot were close in the standings. Every ride counted. Ty couldn't afford even a mediocre ride, meaning it could not be ordinary or average. It came down to a bull named Hard Copy. He kicked and lunged, but Ty hung on. The crowd cheered as they saw the score: Ty Murray had won his seventh title as All-Around Champion. And who was one of the first people to congratulate Ty? None other than Larry Mahan, the great champion himself. "Congratulations, Ty," a gracious Larry told him. "I've known for a lot of years that this night was coming."[5] Ty couldn't have been happier.

Ty is more than just a great athlete who can hang on to bucking broncs and bulls. He is a sharp businessman and was one of the first rodeo athletes to have an agent represent him. He also helped create the Professional Bull Riders, an association that highlights the fan-favorite sport. This is not surprising for a guy many considered the toughest to ride bulls.

The great rodeo writer Ed Knocke lists Ty as one of the five best roughstock riders of all time.

In his book, *King of the Cowboys*, Ty wrote how he wants to be remembered. "I've always wanted to be known as a great cowboy, a good, tough cowboy whose word still means something, and who lives his life in the cowboy way. I don't care about going down in history as a great bull rider or bronc rider. I just hope that when people think back after my career's over, they'll remember me as a great cowboy."[6]

Ty says:

- Ty's favorite book: "My favorite book from when I was a kid was called *10 Karat Hole in a Donut*. It was the life story of a cowboy named Bert France. It was fun to read books that were about the things that I was interested in."
- Ty's inspiration and words of wisdom: "My dad was the biggest inspiration, and I think success is being involved in something you are passionate about. To have an exciting reason to get out of bed every day is more important to happiness than financial gain."
- "The reason my dad was my biggest inspiration is because he taught me how important it is to never weaken."

10 Karat Hole in a Donut is a 1973 book by Billy Wilcoxson. The book details the life of Bert France, an unsung hero and great cowboy in the author's eyes. Wilcoxson quit rodeo to write.

18

VICTOR OLADIPO, BASKETBALL

More Than a Player

Athletes work hard at their sports, but it's important to remember that they are people with interests other than what they do on a field, court, or rink. Victor Oladipo is living proof of that.

You might say Victor was destined to become a basketball player. When she was pregnant with him, his mother, Joan, had a dream that a great player named Hakeem Olajuwon gave a basketball to her child. In 1992, she gave birth to twins, Victor and a girl named Victoria. Victor, his mom said, would carry a basketball everywhere, even before he was in kindergarten.

"That woman believed in me when I was in the womb. Before I was even born," Victor said, calling his mom his "No. 1 fan."[1]

Victor began playing basketball at an early age, attending St. Jerome's Academy in Maryland. High school coaches began looking at the best middle-school kids, hoping they could persuade them to attend their school when they became older. One time, several of these coaches came to St. Jerome's to look at a player named Quinn Cook. He was good and would go on to have a great career, but it was then they discovered Victor.

Victor began attending DeMatha High School, which is well-known for its strong basketball teams. But right before he was to start playing, he broke his foot. Victor didn't want to be away from his teammates and

coaches, so he attended practices, assisted in cleaning up the gym, and helped move chairs. His coaches noticed that spirit.

"His message was 'You guys are not going to forget about me because I'm hurt.' That really endeared him to us," said his high school coach, Mike Jones. [2]

Because his family did not live nearby, he would get up at 4:30 a.m. every day to make it to school by 6 a.m. to practice his shooting before class. Coach Jones said Victor was not arrogant. He would have lunch with nonathletes. "He'd talk to everybody. After a while, everyone knew his name, and nobody was afraid to approach him." [3]

Victor continued to work hard. He averaged almost 12 points, 10 rebounds, and 3.6 blocks per game. In 2009–2010, DeMatha won 32 games, lost only 4, and won the city championship. It was DeMatha's fifth title in six years. Pretty soon, colleges were looking at him. They liked Victor for a few reasons. He had a good reputation off the court, and although he wasn't the best player around, he was a "swingman," which in basketball means he could play two positions—guard and forward. But he also was known as a good defensive player—something coaches at all levels love. Many colleges were interested in Victor, including Notre Dame, Maryland, and Clemson. But he especially liked Indiana University, a pretty campus in Bloomington, which is in the south-central part of the state. The school has a rich tradition in basketball. And he really liked the coach of the Hoosiers, Tom Crean, as well as the school's faithful fans.

Victor started out OK, but it was his work ethic that impressed his coaches. He was usually the last player to leave practice, always working on his game. Soon Victor earned a starting job, and in December 2010 as a freshman he scored 14 points against Penn State. Victor was proving he could play basketball with the best players in college. In one game, he even heaved a 60-foot shot at the end of the first half, which is all the way back near the opposing team's three-point line. The ball went through the basket.

Indiana wasn't good Victor's freshman year. That was a bit of an adjustment for a player who came from a great high school like DeMatha. But his teammates recognized how hard Victor was playing, and after his first season several teammates said they expected him to have the most improved year. They were right; he kept getting better. Against Michigan State his junior year, he scored 19 points and tipped in a key bucket with 43 seconds remaining to lead Indiana to a big win. Even the opposing team's coach, Tom Izzo, praised Victor. "Oladipo is just a refuse-to-lose guy, you know?" he said.[4] Fans often would chant "O-LA-DEEE-PO! O-LA-DEEE-PO!" Victor was averaging close to 14 points per game, and he had 78 steals. He was named the Defensive Player of the Year in his conference. Now, just as college coaches had taken notice when he was in high school, professional scouts were starting to pay attention. The steals in particular were important to them because that showed how defensive-minded Victor could be. Victor, too, knew defense was important.

"I'm not the greatest shooter and I'm not the greatest at certain things, but I do know that I'm going to continue to work at it so I can get there. I have a lot to work on, but I'm going to keep on working until I can perfect it. Because I want to be the best basketball player that I can be," he said.[5]

In 2013, when the National Basketball Association (NBA) Draft rolled around, Victor was ready. He wore a gray suit, black tie, and purple shirt. The Orlando Magic chose Victor with their first pick. He was the second overall player taken.

"My defense is everything. It's the reason why I got here, and it's the reason I'm at the point that I am now, and why it's going to help me separate myself in the future. I'm going to keep growing in that area as well. I feel like I can grow in different aspects of my defense, too, so I'm going to definitely bring that to the Orlando Magic."[6]

Few people were happier for the players selected than Indiana's Coach Crean, who said, "Victor came in and brought his energy and brought his loudness and his happiness, all those things, and then he showed this incredible work ethic to this team. . . . He's an extremely gifted athlete, tremendous charisma and strength of will and personality, but when he gets in the gym, it's all business and that's what propelled him to so many different things."[7] (Charisma is the rare quality that some people have in showing they can be a leader, for drawing the devotion of those around them.)

As good a basketball player as Victor was, he enjoyed things off the court, too. He liked movies—especially the *Home Alone* series, where a boy, Kevin, is accidentally left alone in his family's house during Christmas. His favorite comic-book hero was Wolverine. And he loved singing. His teammates once said he sings everywhere he goes. He particularly likes rhythm and blues.

"I believe there's a song for everything, so anything that reminds me of a song, I'm gonna sing it on the spot. I'm weird. I sing at the spur of the moment. . . . My sisters growing up, they hated it, I mean, not hated it, but I was really annoying because I sang everywhere. That was the only way I could practice. In the shower, anywhere, I used to sing, and they could hear it, so it was kind of annoying to them. But my mom was like, 'My son can sing, my son can sing,' so she always had my back."[8]

Victor's singing became known to a lot of people. One time, he appeared with talk-show host Regis Philbin, and they sang a soul song called "Ain't No Sunshine" by a man named Bill Withers. At a college pep rally he sang Usher's "U Got It Bad."

"Music is my getaway, it's my hobby, it's what I love to do," he said.[9]

One of his agents once called Victor "a dual threat—on and off the court. He has a legitimate and amazing voice. With his passion and knowledge of music, he could be a legitimate R&B star on his own." She turned out to be right, because a few years later Victor put out an album called *V.O.* He collaborated with singers Trey Songz and Tory Lanez. "I feel like sometimes there's a stigma that because I'm an athlete that's the only thing I can do and there's no way I could be good at other things," Victor told a reporter.[10] A stigma is something that carries a longtime negative meaning or belief that is accepted by many people. Victor put out the album on his own music label, called Feathery Music. "Feathery" is a word Victor uses to describe how he is feeling when things are going OK.

When Victor was drafted, he didn't know he eventually would have a national stage to share his singing talents. That would come later. But first, there was a basketball career to get going with the Orlando Magic.

When Victor started working out with Orlando, the team asked something of him: Play point guard. This was interesting because Victor had never played that position in high school or college. Now an NBA team was asking Victor to change positions before he had even played a second of professional ball!

On October 29, 2013, Victor donned his Orlando Magic uniform and made his debut as a professional player. The game turned out to be against the Indiana Pacers, so Victor wasn't far from where he went to college and still had many fans. His team lost, but Victor had a good game, scoring 12 points, with three rebounds and two assists.

Pretty soon it was clear Victor was no ordinary rookie. Coaches often like to let rookies sit on the bench for a while during games so they can watch and learn. But when his coaches let him play almost an entire game against the Chicago Bulls, Victor responded well: He scored a career-high 35 points. He was the first rookie to play that much in a game since two players did it in 1954!

Victor was gaining a reputation as a player who rarely took "possessions off" on defense—meaning, he was a hard worker who never quit on offense or defense. Victor was playing so well he was chosen to participate in the Rising Stars challenge, an All-Star game for young players in the NBA, and the slam-dunk contest. In the game, he scored 22 points. And in the slam-dunk contest, he hit a "540" by spinning his body 1 ½ times around before dunking the ball with his back to the basket. Many former ballplayers attend the All-Star Game festivities each year, and Victor had a chance to speak with some of the game's greatest players, like Bill Russell and Oscar Robertson. He even got a chance to meet Hakeem Olajuwon, the player his mother had dreamed about before Victor was born, and had him autograph a basketball. And, because the All-Star festivities were held in New York City that year, he crooned a few lines from a song called "New York, New York" by a famous singer, Frank Sinatra. The crowd and announcers loved it.

Not long after the All-Star festivities, the Magic played the Phoenix Suns, and Victor had a tremendous game. He scored 38 points—the most ever for him, in high school, college, or the pros—but he recognized it would have been better if his team had won. "At the end of the day, we lost. I know I've got a lot to work on and a lot to get better at, so, hopefully, we can start winning those games."[11] After a game against the Atlanta Hawks, one writer in Orlando wrote, "He ran past the Hawks so fast he gave some of them whiplash."[12] He was joking of course. Whiplash is a spinal injury that occurs often in accidents when someone's head is jerked in a quick motion. But he was pointing out what many writers and commentators noticed: Victor had a lot of energy on the court. He finished that game with 15 points, eight assists, five rebounds, two steals, one block, and five turnovers—a busy day!

In professional sports, trades happen all the time. Teams choose to give up a player at one position to try to strengthen another, weaker area on the team. And as the 2016 NBA Draft was taking place, that's what happened between Oklahoma City and Orlando. The Oklahoma City Thunder sent a star player named Serge Ibaka to Orlando for three players. One of the players was Victor. The trade meant Victor was going from a not-so-great Orlando team to one that was supposed to contend for a championship.

When the Thunder held their annual media day, when players, coaches, and reporters gather before the season, Victor was having fun. He sang, he juggled, and he talked with people he had never met. His new coach would be Billy Donovan, who had been the coach at the University of Florida years earlier and had tried to recruit Victor. But the Thunder didn't live up to their expectations, and the team decided to make some moves at the end of the season. The Thunder surprised almost everyone by announcing they were trading Victor and a player named Domantas Sabonis for Paul George. Victor's new team? The Indiana Pacers. The Pacers played in Indianapolis, about 50 miles from where Victor went to college.

He immediately became a scoring leader for the Pacers, pouring in 35 points in one of his first games.

"Oladipo has been one of the NBA's best shooting guards this young season, and his effort and enthusiasm is consistent," wrote Clifton Brown, who was covering the Pacers for the *Indianapolis Star*.[13] He wrote that Victor was playing like an All-Star and that he had been "a complete player, making a difference at both ends. And his shot selection is much improved over prior seasons."[14] It turned out to be a good prediction: Victor would be named an All-Star that year. The writer noted how good a player Victor was defensively. He also was becoming a leader on the court. "Figuring out the best way to lead can be one of the most difficult obstacles for players who want to be great. But Oladipo seems to be figuring it out—quickly." His coach, Nate McMillan, also praised Victor. "He's just been fun to coach. He absorbs everything that you tell him. He's still a young guy who wants to learn. I've had more film sessions with him than I've had, really with any player. It's because he wants to get better. He wants to improve. He's showing the potential that he has."[15]

In December 2017, the Pacers hosted the Cleveland Cavaliers, who boasted having the great LeBron James. Cleveland had won 13 games in a row, but Victor played well. He scored 33 points, had eight rebounds, and five assists, and the Pacers won, 106–102. In another game, he scored 47 points as his team beat the Denver Nuggets, 126–116, in overtime. After that game, Clifton Brown wrote that Victor "never seems to wear down. It is rare to see Oladipo breathing heavily. . . . (he) acts like he runs on batteries that never need to be charged."[16]

The Pacers played so well they made the playoffs. In his first playoff game, Victor scored 32 points. Indiana played a tough Cleveland team but lost in seven games. Right after the playoffs, Victor tried his hand at being an announcer for TNT. And he was named to the 2018 All-Defensive First Team. "(Defending) was the first thing I could do, before I could even dribble. I wasn't the most skilled, so I had to find a way to play on the court."[17] Victor even played 64 straight games with at least one steal.

Victor had discovered the keys to success on the basketball court. Off of it, he was learning something else: He liked to travel and learn.

Once, in a press conference, he said something about getting used to his teammates, but it's just as true about life: "I just love getting to know new people. I'm just looking forward first and foremost to just getting to know them as people—where they come from, their background, their stories. It's funny 'cause everyone in life is a story. We all have stories in there, we all come from different backgrounds."[18]

In college he had a chance to take a two-week trip to China as part of a cultural exchange project that involved playing basketball. It was his first trip outside of the United States. He visited the Great Wall, the Forbidden City, and Tiananmen Square. The Great Wall is a famous wall created many centuries ago in China as a fortress. It is about 13,000 miles long. Completed in 1420 in China, the Forbidden City is one of the world's largest palaces. It is named because, as the home to 24 emperors over many years, it was forbidden for regular people to visit. Now it is a grand museum that attracts many visitors. And Tiananmen Square is an area in Beijing, China, that in 1989 became the site for an infamous protest by students who wanted their government to be more open. The protests resulted in the government killing many protesters. "Tiananmen" means "gate of heavenly peace."

"A lot of people don't get the opportunity like that to travel across the world, and I'm really glad I was able to do that. We played against great competition and also got to experience a different ethnic background. I'm really glad I went." It didn't hurt that he hit a buzzer-beater on the court in one of the games, either![19]

The NBA also was interested in players competing overseas—specifically, in Africa, where more than 70 players had ties. In 2015, the league held a game in Johannesburg, South Africa. Victor wanted to play in the game, but his schedule didn't allow it. But two years later he got his chance. It was important to him for a special reason. His parents, Chris and Joan, were born in Africa. His dad is from Sierra Leone, and his mom is from Nigeria. "I grew up on it," Victor said. "I grew up listening to the language and listening to the music and eating the food. I'm very familiar with it."[20] Victor visited the Nelson Mandela Museum as well as an orphanage. Nelson Mandela was an influential leader in South Africa who spent many years in a hard-labor prison. He had opposed apartheid, the system of separating people by race in his country. After he was released from prison, he helped change laws to dismantle apartheid policies.

"I've always wanted to come to Africa and be on African soil. To play the game I love and experience a new culture is something I couldn't pass up on," Victor said.[21]

The game matched NBA players from Africa and players of African heritage, like Victor. Victor played well, scoring 28 points while grabbing nine rebounds and five assists to help Team World defeat Team Africa, 108–97. He was named Most Valuable Player.

Life was going well for Victor. Stardom was in his future, a writer said in 2018: "It's just a question of how high his star rises and how brightly it shines."[22] Unfortunately, things were about to change. Victor would have to deal with the biggest challenge he had ever faced.

During his career, Victor suffered occasional injuries, as many athletes of all sports do. He had an aching Achilles tendon, sprained a ligament in his knee, suffered a concussion, and others. Sometimes he would have to miss a few games to heal.

Early in the 2018–2019 season, Victor showed how far he had come as a player when he had a great game in the famed Madison Square Garden against the New York Knicks. He played hard, scoring 11 of his 24 points in the final quarter. And he did it while he was suffering from bronchitis. (Bronchitis is inflammation of the tubes that bring air to the lungs. It can cause wheezing and coughing.) He felt pain in his right knee and ended up missing 11 games in November and December. The team didn't do as well without Victor. Then, on Wednesday, January 23, 2019, Victor's career took an ugly turn.

Indiana hosted the Toronto Raptors, and the first half was almost over. Victor raced up the court after Pascal Siakem, who was trying to score for Toronto. Suddenly, Victor collapsed. His right leg had given out, and he lay on the court. Right away everyone—teammates and fans—knew it was serious. Victor screamed as he held his leg. Victor was taken to the locker room on a stretcher. The crowd went silent. Victor had ruptured his right quadriceps tendon. Soon, surgery was scheduled to reattach tendons to his kneecap.

"That kid has a beautiful spirit," said his coach, Nate McMillan. "He is the most positive guy on this team. He has always been one to try to lift his team, lift us. We got to lift him now. We have to support him now in this time."[23]

Knee injuries are common in sports because of the wear and tear athletes endure while running, especially in constant stop-and-start motion. But a "right quad" injury is fairly rare. When you straighten your knee, you are using your quadriceps tendons and muscles. Tearing a quadriceps tendon is not common among professional basketball players. Actually, the injury happens more often in older people who slip on ice rather than healthy basketball players. Fans loved watching Victor play so much that the average ticket price for Pacers games actually went down after he was injured. Television networks started airing other teams instead of Indiana. Without Victor, ratings dropped.

After surgery Victor concentrated on rehabilitating his knee. He worked out for three or more hours Monday through Friday and some Saturdays. And he also had to prepare himself mentally to stay positive.

> Your mind is another muscle you need to work on through this process. A lot of people don't train their mind. That's what I'm focused on the most. . . . I'm a positive butterfly. I thrive off positivity, and I kind of preach it. I'm real big on my faith and my belief in God, and at the end of the day how can I say that and act that way every day and then when I'm at my lowest point I shy away from that? I wouldn't be practicing what I preach. . . . I am human. It hasn't been easy. There's been tough days, there have been days that have been tougher than other days. But for the most part I have survived every single one of them. So when I say I'm coming back better than ever I'm not just saying that because it sounds good, it's because I truly believe that. It's because of the God I serve, that's it.[24]

Something positive came out of Victor's time away from the court: More people discovered his ability to sing. Weeks before Victor injured his knee, Fox debuted a show called *The Masked Singer*. In it singers were disguised by elaborate costumes. They would sing wearing the costumes, and judges would try to guess who they were. They were given names like Ladybug and Watchamacallit. After the songs a host would ask questions to the disguised performers, and they would give clues— with their voice disguised—to aid the judges.

When the show began its season, one of the performers went by the name Thingamajig. Many of the clues for this character sounded like it could be Victor. Thingamajig mentioned the number 4, which is Victor's jersey number as well as his birthday—he was born May 4. He also said "magic" in his clues, and the Orlando Magic was the first NBA team he played for. He also referred to sign language, and many people might not have known it but Victor's oldest sister, Kendra, is deaf. Each week people tuned in to watch and guess who the singers were. Even sports reporters started paying attention and asked Victor about it. At first Victor denied it was him. He had to keep the secret. But then the time came on the show for the singer to take off the crazy costume head, a yellow fuzzy, glasses-wearing top. The character slowly reached up as the crowd and judges waited and . . . it was Victor! Judges said he had a natural voice they really liked.

Later, Victor said, "If I could encourage a little kid who has a dream, I would also say you can achieve any dream you want. Just know that that feeling that you have that you know you can do it but it's like no one else thinks you can, all that matters is that you know you can. I'm living proof of it."[25]

Victor also proved he could play basketball again. On January 29, 2020, after just more than a year away from the sport, he returned in a game on the same court where he was injured. He scored nine points, and while he might not have been 100 percent he made a crucial three-point shot to tie the game with 10 seconds remaining. The Pacers went on to win, and Victor left the court with a big smile.

While Victor played he also kept an eye on other business interests. In 2020, he launched a clothing line with a company called Express. Then, he and a business manager of his decided to become part owners of the New Zealand Breakers, a team that plays in the Australian National Basketball League. Players cannot own a team in the league they play in; that would be a conflict of interest. That's a position that favors someone unfairly. If a player were to own another team in his or her league, that would put them in an odd position when the team they played for competed against the team they owned. And it is not common for a present-day athlete to own a team in another league. But Victor felt the time was right. Being a businessman was as important to him as being a singer, understanding his heritage in Africa, launching a clothing line, or doing anything else he puts his mind to.

In January 2021 a big trade happened in the NBA. It involved four teams swapping several players and draft picks. And Victor was one of those players. He would now be a member of the Houston Rockets. But not long after the deal, Victor was traded to the Miami Heat. Unfortunately, while playing for Miami, Victor suffered another injury—to the same part of his leg he had injured in 2019. No matter what team Victor plays for, he wants one thing to be clear.

"At the end of the day we aren't just athletes. . . . being an athlete is not just dribbling the ball or throwing a football or kicking a soccer ball. There's so much more that we have to do outside of that."[26]
Victor says:

- Victor's favorite book growing up: "Dr. Seuss, all of them. They were colorful, educational and easy to read."
- Victor's words of wisdom: "What I learned is the key to success is hard work." He added: "I had to overcome some things in life in general. Growing up, you face a lot of obstacles. People doubted me, but it made me stronger to prove them wrong. My inspiration came from my mother and my sisters. They never doubted what I could become and were with me every step of the way."

The Dr. Seuss series was written by Theodor Seuss "Ted" Geisel (1904–1991). In 1957, he published one of his most famous books, How the Grinch Stole Christmas! *It was turned into a popular animated show that airs on television in December even to this day.*

19

CAT OSTERMAN, SOFTBALL
The Untouchable Tall Texan

T*hump!* The ball fired into the catcher's mitt for strike one. The pitcher gripped the ball in front of her, wound up, and threw—another swing and a miss. Strike two. The pitcher kicked some dirt and eyed her catcher. The batter dug her cleats in to the batter's box and waited. The pitcher brought her left arm above her and then rocketed the ball toward home plate. It came in waist high but then, suddenly, the ball rose and twisted a little bit. The batter lunged. Off balance, she missed. Not even close. Strike three, she was out!

For Cat Osterman, it was just another day on the mound.

Before you could say "Catherine Leigh Osterman," one of Cat's pitches would be across the plate. And most of the time, it would be in the catcher's mitt after a batter swung and missed.

One of the greatest softball pitchers ever grew up in Texas and loved sports. Basketball was her favorite. She played goalie in soccer, but her team was so good she saw little action and became bored. In fifth grade, her softball team was in a tournament, and the coach wanted to give the regular pitchers a break. Cat volunteered and found a new love: pitching. She asked for lessons, and soon, if anyone wanted to find Cat Osterman, it was on a nearby mound.

"I'm not away from softball unless I'm eating or sleeping," Cat once said.[1]

Gary Osterman knew his daughter could be good. Gary painted two lines 40 feet apart on the family's driveway to mark the distance between the mound and home plate. At 14, Cat worked hard, and soon she learned to develop pitches. Some pitchers in softball and baseball rely on speed. But Cat depended on something else: movement. Her pitches, she learned with practice, could dip or rise, twist and turn, making it difficult for batters to hit. "I would never let her get on a radar gun," her dad once said. "We concentrated on spin."[2] A radar gun isn't really a gun; it's a device that measures the speed of a pitched ball or moving object.

In eighth grade, two things happened that would stay with Cat forever. On her volleyball team, there were so many girls with names like "Kathy" and "Katie" that she started going by "Cat," which she still does. And in English class she wrote a story about pitching for the University of Texas, chalking up strikeouts in a championship game. Softball was now a big priority in her life. At Cypress Springs High School near Houston, she once struck out all 21 batters she faced. Another time, she recorded 33 strikeouts in an extra-inning game. It lasted 14 innings, and Cat didn't allow a run. For all her efforts, Cat was named the national player of the year.

While she was 17 and in high school, Cat was part of a special squad that got a chance to scrimmage the US National team, who were gearing up for the 2000 Olympics. It was a hot July day in Texas. If Cat were nervous, she didn't show it. Over five innings, she faced 16 batters and struck out 11. No one scored, and only one batter got a hit off her. "She definitely was on their radar after that," said her mom, Laura.[3]

"What stays with me is the picture of this tall, skinny kid just throwing the heck out of the ball. Her ball moved like no one's I'd ever seen," said Lori Harrigan, one of the Olympians.[4]

When it came time for college, it wasn't too hard a choice for Cat. She chose her beloved University of Texas Longhorns in the state capital, Austin. And she kept up her winning ways.

Major League baseball pitchers often throw 90 miles per hour or more. Some even approach 100. Cat was throwing 62 to 66 miles per hour. The big difference, though, is that baseball pitchers are 60 feet, 6 inches from home. In softball, the pitcher and batter are only 43 feet apart. Cat used this to her advantage. She knew batters had no time to decide which pitch was coming, so she surprised them. She threw two types of curve balls, and she learned how to make a pitch drop or rise. And she even threw a screwball, which turns the opposite way of a curve. "I'm more of a finesse pitcher," Cat once said.[5]

That type of pitching confused opposing teams. Over four years, while sporting the burnt orange uniform with the Longhorn logo, Cat was one of the nation's most dominant pitchers. In her freshman year, 2002, the 6 foot 2 Cat struck out 554 batters. In 2005, she struck out 16 Missouri Tigers to help Texas win the Big 12 title. In an NCAA Baseball Tournament game two weeks later, 17 players whiffed as Cat led the Longhorns past the Crimson Tide of Alabama. Of all the great games and moments Cat had in college, two things stand out: She was the first pitcher at Texas to throw a perfect game—she wound up with 10 of them in college—and she is one of only three collegiate pitchers ever to record more than 2,000 strikeouts. In fact, Cat holds an incredible record: She struck out more than 14 players per game.

Perfect games are difficult to achieve because they take a lot of concentration as well as athletic effort. It means no one gets on base, ever. In a seven-inning game, a pitcher must retire 21 consecutive batters. In 2002, in the first game of a doubleheader against Stephen F. Austin University, Cat earned her first perfect game. (A doubleheader is when softball or baseball teams play back-to-back games.) Then her coach called on her in the second game. She allowed only one hit and won again! During another perfect game, against Baylor, Cat broke her right thumb—and still didn't allow a base runner. Against Oklahoma State her freshman year, Cat was perfect and had extra reason to celebrate. It was the Big 12 Championship Game. "I think I was celebrating the conference championship more than the perfect game. A lot of the team didn't realize we had a perfect game going," she said.

"When you look at her stats, you shake your head. Years from now people will remember her name," said her Texas coach, Connie Clark, who was a great pitcher once herself.[6]

It was significant that Cat once told a reporter one of her favorite movies was *For Love of the Game*. In the 1999 movie, Kevin Costner plays a baseball pitcher who is trying to throw a perfect game.

Opposing players didn't forget who the tall Texan pitcher was. Neither did the officials with the US National Team. In 2004, she became the youngest member on the squad, at age 21. With the national team Cat would play in two Olympics, winning gold in 2004 and silver in 2008. Olympic players got to choose what music they wanted to hear while they warmed up before pitching. Cat chose a popular song at the time called "Can't Be Touched." That was fitting for Cat, who allowed just one hit in her debut game as an Olympian. While she competed in Athens, Greece, in the 2004 Games, the time-zone change made it tough to watch games back home. But Cat's Texas teammates dragged themselves out of bed at 4 a.m. to see her on television. And when she returned to the United States, they all greeted her at the airport. In the 2004 Games, Cat joined with Lisa Fernandez and Jennie Finch to form what some people considered the three best pitchers on one team anywhere in the world. All eventually would play professional softball.

Cat had helped put softball on the map, and people took notice. Many high school athletes all over the country chose her as their favorite athlete. She became the first softball player to appear on the cover of *Sports Illustrated*. She earned the Big 12 Athlete of the Year award three times. And she was named Female Athlete of the Year by ESPN, which awarded her an ESPY. The ESPY award was especially valued by Cat, because *SportsCenter* is one of her favorite television shows.

"It's been kind of interesting to watch (Cat's popularity) grow over the years. She has this rock-star status. It's pretty amazing, and it's amazing the type of ambassador she has become for the game of softball. She handles it well," Coach Clark once said.[7] An ambassador is a messenger or representative, usually of a government or country. More informally, it can be someone who is good at what he or she does and proudly, but not boastfully, represents it.

After college and the Olympics, Cat played professional softball, but deep down she always knew she wanted to coach. So she went back to college to instruct young players. It's a perfect fit for Cat, who believes accomplishments don't just happen in the game, they begin in practice.

In fact, Cat wants people to know that it took a lot of practice and determination to achieve what she did on the field.

"What I'd like for people to remember is that it was a lot of hard work. There's never been a day I stopped working at being as perfect as I can with this craft."[8]

One time a reporter talked to Jean Joyce, a great pitcher in the 1960s and 1970s. Jean was blunt: "Truth be told, Cat Osterman may be the best ever."[9]

Who better to teach young women to be great softball players?

Cat says:

- Cat's favorite books: "When I was younger my favorite books were the Madeline series. I used to make my mom read them to me, and we read them so much that I memorized the books and would read ahead of her. I loved the book fair and reading contests at school. Even as an adult I love to escape to the world of reading when I have time. I love reading!"
- Cat's words of wisdom: "During my career, I learned how hard work and determination can go a long way. I didn't really run into any obstacles, but I learned that if I want something I need to work hard to get it. My dad pushed me to work hard, so anytime I practiced I gave 100% and never any less. I loved what I did so it was easy to continue to work to be the best I could be!"

Madeline is a series of books by Ludwig Bemelmans (1898–1962) that follows a small, but brave, little girl in a boarding school in Paris. The series was first published in 1939.

20

LYN ST. JAMES, AUTO RACING

From Student to Teacher

Long before Lyn St. James slid behind the wheel of a fast racing machine to zoom around at speeds well above 200 miles per hour, she sat, still, for long periods of time.

That's because Lyn's first love was the piano. She practiced and became a teacher. But deep inside she had a passion to race. It might have been in her blood because her mom was a taxicab driver in World War II. Or maybe she learned to like it by working in a gas station, as she did for a summer job growing up in Willoughby, Ohio. Her mom taught her to drive, and the two of them went on long road trips together. Whatever it was, Lyn knew she wanted to race.

Lyn was born Evelyn Cornwall, but she changed her name to Lyn St. James—"Lyn" comes from her given first name, and "St. James" is from the name of Susan St. James, an actress who starred on an old television show called *McMillan and Wife* that Lyn liked.

Two of Lyn's early races stand out for different outcomes. When she was 17, Lyn and some friends went to a drag race to see a friend compete in Louisville, Kentucky. That's a race between cars that start from a standing position. Whoever crosses the finish line first wins. When he lost, Lyn told him he didn't drive right. The friend snapped: "Why don't you drive it then?" So she did—and she won. When she arrived home, trophy in hand, her mother wasn't happy. After all, she had taught Lyn to drive safe, not to be a speed demon.

The other race came several years later, when Lyn had moved to Florida and was driving a Pinto. The squat car made by Ford was popular for a while early in the 1970s. So Lyn went to a driving school and learned to become a race-car driver. She entered a race on a South Florida course that had little ponds and water holes all around the track. The course even had divers standing by in case a driver crashed and became stuck in the car under water. Lyn started out well in her car, which had a giant "X" on it, meaning she was a rookie driver. She zipped around the course, feeling confident. She turned well along the curves, but what she didn't realize was that the fastest cars in the race had lapped her. That meant they now were coming up behind her, and Lyn forgot to do something important. She forgot to check her mirrors. All of a sudden, a car sped past her. Startled, Lyn spun out, leaving the asphalt of the track. She felt herself swing into the grassy area and then she came to a stop. She scrambled out of the car into a murky mess, then heard an awful noise: "Blub, blub, blub." The car was sinking! Lyn didn't know how to swim, so she scrambled out as best she could. She spent the entire weekend drying out the car, even putting parts in the oven and using a hair dryer to evaporate the water. Days later, whenever Lyn would turn on the fan in the car, bits of seaweed would fly out. Later, at the banquet of the sports club that Lyn belonged to, awards were given to the drivers. Surprisingly, she heard her name called. But she hadn't won a race, she thought, so what award could this be? The club gave her the "Alligator Award" for driving into the lake.

But Lyn kept at it and officially became a professional race-car driver in 1979, coincidentally the last year Janet Guthrie drove in the Indianapolis 500. Janet was the first woman to drive in the prestigious race. But Lyn didn't just jump from small tracks in South Florida to Indianapolis. She competed in races all over, winning *Autoweek* magazine's Rookie of the Year honors. She learned so much about cars and how they work that in 1984 she wrote a car manual for women. A year later, she became the first woman to win a professional race in Watkins Glen, a famous track in upstate New York. In fact, she set 13 national and international speed records for women in 1985. *McCall's* magazine even named her Woman of the Year in 1986.

Lyn knew other drivers and race-car team owners. She approached a man named Dick Simon, a racer and car owner, about moving into Indy-style racing. Dick promised her a ride but time went by. Then, the day after a race in Florida, Lyn got a call from Dick. He told her to be in Memphis, Tennessee, the next morning if she wanted to try out a car on a track. She was ecstatic! Lyn quickly figured out how to get from Florida to Memphis in a hurry. She arrived at the track, slipped behind the wheel, and started up the engine. Of course, the first thing it did was stall. Then she got going, amazed at the power of the 1,800-pound racer. Not used to handling this car, she almost crashed into the wall. But she finished her tryout and impressed Dick and his crew with her driving skills. Later, he took everyone out to dinner, and Lyn recognized the value of teamwork. The members of Dick's crew, she realized, didn't let their egos get in the way of the job they had to do together. Being egotistic means having a tendency to speak of oneself boastfully.

Lyn learned two valuable lessons she would never forget: "You never know what can happen till you ask," she says in her autobiography.[1] This was important because had she not approached Dick, he might never have offered her a chance. And she knew she would have to ask a lot of folks for sponsorship money, a big part of being a professional race-car driver.

She also learned about the value of teamwork. In racing, there is an owner, a crew chief, mechanics, and other support staff. Even though fans may follow a driver, it takes the efforts of many people to keep the car running well. "We all must rely on help from others at varying points in our lives and careers," Lyn wrote. "You can't do it alone; you need to build your successes with a solid team of people who believe in you."[2]

How a car runs and feels to a driver is important. A driver has to feel what the car is telling them—how does it sound? Is it leaning one way or the other? Then the driver must relay those impressions to the team, so they can make adjustments. Every technical adjustment has to be exact, right down to making a custom seat to fit the driver. Even the clothing a driver wears is specially made. Everything, including their socks, is fire-retardant.

Drivers and their teams aim to be in the 33-car Indy 500 field, but first they must qualify. That means each driver gets a chance to go out on the track, one by one, and make four laps. The average speed of those laps is qualifying time. The fastest qualifying times make the field. A big black pole on the track flashes numbers of cars that have qualified. One time Lyn was driving well in qualifying, then all of a sudden the back end of the car slid and she bounced off the inside wall, then hit the outside wall, and finally landed with a thud. Even though she had been in the crash she knew to take off the steering wheel and place it so emergency crews could see it. This is important because it is a sign to medical crews that the driver is alert and not unconscious. It wasn't Lyn's only crash in her career. In a race in Riverside, California, she suffered two herniated discs, cracked ribs, bruises, and she lost the use of her left arm for a little while. A hernia occurs when a body part, like a disc along the spine, protrudes out of alignment.

In the 1996 Indy 500, she broke her wrist, and it took a long time to heal. But drivers simply cannot think about crashes. If they dwelled on the bad things that could happen in a race, they would lose their concentration. Instead, what Lyn learned to do is what many great athletes do in their sports. It's called "visualization." This is when athletes envision accomplishing what they have to do. A soccer player might picture a penalty kick going past the goalie. A race-car driver would think about each and every turn in a race. Throughout her career, Lyn worked hard to keep negative thoughts away. As she once said, "Winners prepare to win."[3]

When she wasn't on the track Lyn was seeking money from sponsors. Without companies willing to sponsor them, racing teams would not be able to pay for parts for their cars. And parts could be expensive. When Lyn was driving, an engine alone was $100,000! Lyn's requests were turned down a lot. In 1992, she figured she received 150 rejections. Many companies didn't want to sponsor a woman driver because they felt most racing fans were men. But some companies came to believe in her. A bagel company sponsored her. A clothing company called Stinky Feet also supported her. In 1992, Lyn's first of seven Indy 500s, JC Penney gave Lyn's team money, and they called her car *The Spirit of the American Woman*. Lyn was the oldest rookie in the race at age 45, and she finished 11th. She also was the second woman ever to race in the Indy 500.

A big moment in racing history came in 2000 when, for the first time, the Indy 500 had two women racing. Lyn and a young woman named Sarah Fisher made the field. Lyn was the oldest driver in the race at age 53, and Sarah was the youngest at 19. It also was the first time the track announcer ever said, "Ladies and gentlemen, start your engines!" Unfortunately, Lyn, Sarah, and a driver named Jaques Lazier collided on lap 74, and both women did not finish.

What is interesting is that Sarah Fisher has Lyn St. James in part to thank for her racing career. Lyn had decided long ago she would start a driver-development program to train young women who wanted to race cars. Hundreds went through the program, including Sarah and a young driver who would become a fan favorite, Danica Patrick.

Lyn had become a teacher. She remembered the chance Dick Simon gave her. "I wouldn't be accomplishing what I have if not for Dick and Dianne Simon. You have to have people who believe in you; I don't care who you are."[4] Now here she was helping others with her driving program.

Lyn once told a reporter, "Many male drivers told me, 'I couldn't do what you do.' But the car doesn't know the difference. It's a gender-neutral sport."[5]

Lyn has always stressed learning. "I read books, asked plenty of questions, and tried to learn from drivers and teams that were winning. You never can stop learning," she once said.[6]

In 2001, Lyn took a few special laps around the Indy 500 track, becoming the first driver that year to drive the track right before the race. She had decided she no longer would compete, that these laps would mark her final ones. She used her time wisely, though, testing the car for her crew and telling them what felt right and wrong. She had learned so much as both a student and teacher in auto racing, and her last act at Indy would be to help her crew one final time.

"Through sports I've learned that everything in life is like a game. First you have to learn the rules, then learn to play by the rules, then learn to win by the rules," she said.[7]

Lyn once told a reporter her advice for drivers coming after her in the sport: "Now is all you've got. Go for it!"[8]

Lyn says:

- Lyn's favorite books: "When I was a child I honestly don't remember reading that many books other than what was required reading. I was more interested in *doing* than reading about others—between school, sports and music—I was busy. Now I thoroughly enjoy reading—especially biographies and autobiographies. On my book shelf: Charles Lindbergh, Anne Morrow Lindbergh, Amelia Earhart, Warren Buffett, Anita Roddick . . . Queen Noor, Tom Peters, Isak Dinesen, Sandra Day O'Connor and many others, including many athletes. My favorite book (which is out of print) is *The Magic of Believing*, by Claude Bristol."

Charles Lindbergh (1902–1974) flew a solo flight from New York to Paris in 1927. It was the first solo flight across the Atlantic Ocean. Anne Morrow Lindbergh (1906–2001) married Charles in 1929. Amelia Earhart (1897–1937?) was an aviation pioneer who became the first woman to fly solo across the Atlantic Ocean. Warren Buffett (1930–) is a wealthy investor and philanthropist, a person who gives away money to various causes. Anita Roddick (1942–2007) was a British woman who founded a cosmetics company called The Body Shop in 1976. Queen Noor (1951–) is a US-born woman who became part of the royal family in the country of Jordan in the Middle East. She was married to King Hussein (1935–1999), and she is involved in many charitable works. Tom Peters (1942–) writes and speaks on how businesses can improve their communication skills. Isak Dinesen (1885–1962) was the pen name for Danish author Karen Blixen. Sandra Day O'Connor (1930–) was the first woman to serve on the US Supreme Court. Claude Bristol (1891–1951) was a soldier and journalist who wrote inspirational books about positive thinking.

21

DICK SCHULTZ, SPORTS EXECUTIVE

The Man in Charge

Younger athletes often dream of going on to a big college career in their sport or starring as a professional. Others don't play but love sports, so they find ways to stay associated with the games they love.

Dick Schultz did both.

Growing up in Kellogg, Iowa, a town of a few hundred in central Iowa in the 1930s and 1940s, Dick did what a lot of kids then did: He played sports. "When you grow up in a small Iowa community, that's just kind of expected."[1] His parents were raised on farms, as were many folks in the Hawkeye State. Not having siblings to play with meant Dick had more time for sports. He especially loved baseball. Field conditions were tough—there were no dugouts, no baseline fences, and teams had one uniform for both home and away games. But the local field had something that was new and important—lights. That meant Dick and his friends could play longer hours. Dick became good as a catcher and outfielder. Friends said he could run "like the wind."[2] He also played in the band in his tiny high school, which had only 16 or 17 students in his graduating class. When it came time to go to college, Dick chose Central College in Pella, about 30 miles south. There he continued to show his love for sports the only way he knew how, by playing them. He ran a kickoff back in football almost the entire length of the field. In basketball, he once hit a last-second shot. By the time Dick had graduated in 1950, he had earned 10 varsity letters in three sports.

Dick did something else in college that was important. He got married after his junior year to his sweetheart, Jackie. Soon, Dick had an important decision to consider. The St. Louis Browns, a Major League Baseball team, were interested in him. They offered him a contract for $350 a month, plus a $3,000 signing bonus. That was a lot of money back then. But the minor-league team that Dick was supposed to report to did not allow wives or families to come along. Dick decided not to go, and any chance of playing in the Majors ended right then. Instead, he took a job coaching and teaching biology at a high school in Humboldt, Iowa. He and Jackie lived in a trailer, and she taught in a one-room schoolhouse. Dick had always enjoyed coaching, beginning when he was a senior in high school helping seventh- and eighth-graders play basketball. He eventually moved on to the University of Iowa, where he coached baseball and basketball. As much as Dick loved coaching, he felt there was a life span to the profession. He had seen coaches become overwhelmed by their work, and he didn't want to suffer "burnout." Burnout means a couple of things. It could be a failure in a device attributed to excessive heat. In a person, it often means someone who works hard at a job, hobby, or sport for a certain period of time and then becomes too tired to continue or needs a break.

So he left coaching in 1974 and went to work for the president of the university. Soon, though, an opportunity came that would bring him back to sports.

Dick was hired as athletic director at Cornell University, an Ivy League school in Upstate New York. There he didn't concentrate on just one or two sports, like when he was playing or coaching; now he was in charge of all the sports. He was becoming an administrator in charge. He was learning things and making decisions that affected the school teams. Sometimes decisions made for the right reasons may not look so good at the time or down the road. That happened not long after Dick arrived at Cornell. The school's football coach had a horrible record: 3–15 in two years. Dick felt he had no choice but to fire the coach. Evaluating coaches is part of the job of an athletic director (AD). The coach was George Seifert, and he eventually went on to a great career as head coach of the San Francisco 49ers in the National Football League (NFL). But Dick kept at it, and eventually the University of Virginia, a larger school in the Atlantic Coast Conference, hired him as AD.

Often one job leads to a bigger one, like when Dick went from Cornell to Virginia. He had no idea at the time, but the next job he would take would be the biggest of all in college sports. The organization that oversees college sports is the National Collegiate Athletic Association (NCAA). The group's first executive director, Walter Byers, announced he would retire in 1987, so a successor was sought. Someone recommended Dick, and a search committee contacted him. He had to give this a lot of thought. He liked his position at Virginia; this was a huge step. To be the top man at the NCAA would be like running a company of 200 people. Dick decided to apply. It turned out he was among 80 people nominated. The committee liked Dick, and they liked that he had a solid sports background. He became one of four finalists. Then it was made official: On October 1, 1987, Dick Schultz was named executive director of the NCAA.

Only one man, Walter Byers, had led the NCAA, and he had done it from 1951 until 1987. His style was different than Dick's. Where Walter liked to stay in his office, Dick liked to travel to meet folks. Dick was a pilot, and it was a skill that helped him quickly get from NCAA headquarters in Kansas to places all over the country. In 1988, he spent 163 days away from home for his job, and 59 of those were spent visiting schools.

Dick immediately had his hands full. After all, there were about 1,000 colleges in the NCAA. Many people turn on the television and see a big college basketball game during March Madness or watch college football in the fall, but those are just two of many sports. They are on TV because people like Dick Schultz helped negotiate deals with television networks to get the games broadcast. He once was involved in getting NCAA basketball games shown on CBS in a deal that brought in $1 billion! In fact, about 300,000 athletes were competing in college sports when Dick was in charge. But there are many other college sports being played throughout fall and spring. Some you might see occasionally on a sports channel or during the Olympics, like gymnastics, track and field, wrestling, field hockey, and volleyball, among many others. The job as executive director of the NCAA is difficult because the person in charge has to oversee all these sports but doesn't have much power.

"Dick is a natural leader," Jim Delaney, a fellow sports executive, once told a reporter. "He's low-key when he chairs meetings, but everyone is aware of who's in charge."[3]

What couldn't Dick do in his job as head of the NCAA? He couldn't throw out anyone for violating one of the many rules. He couldn't suspend or fine anyone for breaking a rule. He just didn't have a "magic wand" to fix problems. What he could do was use "the power of persuasion," he once said.[4] He needed to convince member schools that certain changes were good for college sports. For instance, he wanted to limit the time athletes were allowed to practice. He also wanted to make graduation rates of athletes public, so people could see how many student-athletes were staying in school and getting an education. And he wanted to establish minimum grades for athletes to have to play sports. The integrity and image of the NCAA, Dick said, were his priorities. Many people have heard the expression, "One bad apple spoils the bunch." Well, when an athlete makes a bad choice and is arrested, it makes headlines. But Dick pointed out there were only a few athletes getting into trouble like that. Actually, he said, 98.5 percent of student-athletes were not getting into trouble with drugs or other problems.

One reason Dick was able to make changes was his optimistic outlook. He once said, "To me, the glass has always been half full, not half empty."[5] He also knew hard work paid off, no matter where you come from. "A lot of people think you have to be from the big city. But you can come from a small town and if you apply yourself, have people provide good training and work hard, you have a chance to do whatever you want to do."[6]

Dick led the NCAA for seven years. It was discovered that some athletes at Virginia violated a rule about receiving loans while Dick was the AD there years earlier. Even though he said he was not aware of the violations, he felt he should step down from his post at the NCAA. He felt that his insistence on integrity should start with him.

About a year later, another job in the world of sports administration opened. Again, it was a big one. The US Olympic Committee—the USOC—spent nine months looking for a new executive director. More than 150 applicants applied, and it came down to three finalists. Dick got the job. "We could not have found a better person to tackle the challenges (we have)," another USOC executive, LeRoy Walker, told a reporter.[7] Many sports fans don't think about the Olympics until the games roll around, but the USOC has to make sure US athletes in two dozen sports are supported through proper training programs every year. Dick was in charge of the USOC for five years before retiring. He and his wife Jackie enjoyed building homes; she would design them, and Dick helped build them. The Schultzes retired to Colorado.

At his last NCAA convention, in 1994, Dick addressed the crowd and said he hoped he would be remembered for one thing above all: "When this is all over, if you can't say anything else, I hope you can say 'He made a difference.'"[8]

Dick says:

- Dick's favorite books: "Reading is very important for people of any age, especially children, as it opens our minds to worlds that we may never expect to see, or establish interest in a subject or profession that will lead us to exciting new opportunities."
- "As a child I read many books designed for children my age that involved sports, sports heroes as well as novels about sports competition and the importance of ethical competition. This eventually led me to nearly 50 years of involvement in sports and to some opportunities that I never dreamed about even as a college graduate. Had the interest in sports not been instilled in me by the books I read as a child many of these opportunities would have never happened."
- Dick's inspiration: "My main encouragement in reading came from both parents and both were very encouraging of me as my character and career developed. My college coaches also provided much support and encouragement as I developed my skills."
- Dick's words of wisdom: "Never underestimate the ideas that come to you as you read or the encouragement and motivation you receive from others, especially your parents."

22

ANDRE THORNTON, BASEBALL

Keeping the Faith

We all have obstacles that come our way in life. Andre Thornton had one of the toughest to overcome.

Andre was born in Alabama in 1949. His dad, Harold, played semiprofessional baseball and had a game on the day Andre was born. His father actually asked his mother to hold off giving birth until after the game! Soon, the Thorntons—like many African Americans at the time—moved north for work. Andre was raised in Phoenixville, Pennsylvania, about 30 miles northwest of Philadelphia. He had six brothers and sisters. His father was a machinist, and his mother cleaned people's homes. Andre played football, baseball, and basketball, with football being his best sport.

Andre wasn't a perfect kid growing up. As a youngster, he would bet money shooting pool, and he had a few run-ins with police. But he had two influences in his life that kept him out of serious trouble: His mother, who was religious, and baseball.

Over his career Andre played a lot of positions. He was a shortstop in Little League and in high school. He caught the eye of the Philadelphia Phillies, who drafted him as a third baseman but moved him to first base. He also became serious about a girl named Gert. He and Gert were in love, and they married when Andre was 21. The newlywed couple would find themselves on the move over the next few years. Like many young players, Andre found himself being sent from team to team. First, the

Phillies—who were loaded with first basemen—sent him to Atlanta. Then the Braves traded him to the Chicago Cubs. By now he and Gert had a little boy named Andre, and the family kept moving from town to town. They were becoming a baseball family. Because Andre had not made it to the big leagues yet, he was playing for Class AAA teams in the minor leagues. So the trading merry-go-round sent Andre from Richmond, Virginia, to Wichita, Kansas. Finally, though, Andre started pounding home runs, and the Cubs brought him up to play. He had finally made it.

After almost four seasons in Chicago, the Cubs dealt him to Montreal, where he finished the 1976 season. The moves just kept coming for Andre and his young family. Then, on December 10, 1976, the Montreal Expos traded Andre to the Cleveland Indians. The Indians needed a bat, and the Expos wanted a pitcher. So Cleveland swapped Jackie Brown for Andre Thornton. The next year would be Jackie's final one in a Major League uniform, but for Andre Thornton, the future was just starting.

When Andre landed in Cleveland he felt like he was given a "new beginning."[1] So rather than bouncing between apartments and cities, he and his family established roots. They joined a church and settled into their home in a Cleveland suburb. Andre Jr. now had a baby sister, Theresa. After the 1977 season, Andre's first in Cleveland, he and his family decided to visit Pennsylvania in the off-season. Gert's sister was getting married, and the Thorntons looked forward to the wedding.

It was a trip that would change Andre's life forever.

On October 17, 1977, Andre drove the family van across Pennsylvania, normally a scenic trip in the fall, with trees displaying beautifully colored leaves. When they were almost halfway there, the weather turned nasty. A storm quickly blew in from the Allegheny Mountains, which is part of the Appalachian mountain system in Virginia, West Virginia, Maryland, and central Pennsylvania. They are also known as "the Alleghenies."

Gusts created a wind tunnel, making driving difficult. Snow mixed with freezing rain didn't help. Conditions were definitely dangerous. Andre had the wipers on at full speed, but it didn't help much. Suddenly, the van slid to the right and smashed into the guardrail.

When help arrived, Andre and his 4-year-old son were taken to the hospital. But his 2-year old daughter and 29-year-old wife did not survive. Andre's first instinct in the hospital was to pray, his faith holding him up in his saddest moment. "My faith is the cornerstone of my life. It drives what I do, drives what I believe, and gives me the hope to carry on day by day no matter what I go through."[2] People from all over, even baseball teams, sent flowers. Letters arrived constantly. Eventually, Andre would return to Cleveland to raise his son and play baseball again.

Four months later, he found himself at spring training. While Andre had always kept himself in good physical shape, mentally he was not ready. But he continued to rely on his faith. A few years earlier, Andre had decided that he wanted to live a good life, be a Christian first, and be known as a ballplayer second. But he also knew baseball was his job. Soon, the 1978 season started, and Andre started hitting home runs. He finished the year with 28, more than any one on the team. It was a sign of things to come. Andre would lead the Indians in home runs for seven seasons.

Andre worked hard to stay in shape. Since the early 1970s, Andre had lifted weights. Now, conditioning is more common among ballplayers, but Andre knew to build up his body. In fact, in 1982, a Cleveland coach, Tom McGraw, once told a reporter, "I think he's the strongest man in all of baseball right now. Maybe in all of major sport."[3]

Even though Cleveland finished near the bottom of the division almost every year when Andre was playing, the fans warmed up to the man known as "Thunder." "I really think the tragedy cemented me to the team and the fans in this area," he once told a writer.[4]

Andre's nickname was one of the more colorful ones in baseball. When Andre hit a home run, writers liked to say things like "Thunder strikes again." Once, in a game against Kansas City, Andre hit two home runs and then the skies opened and rain poured. Royals' manager Dick Howser said, "Thornton provided the thunder before Mother Nature did."[5]

How Andre got the nickname is debatable. Some said it was because of his power to hit homers. Maybe it was because one of Andre's brothers had the same nickname. When Andre was a boy, there was a football player named Bill Thornton, who played at the University of Nebraska. Bill's high school coach gave him the nickname back in the 1950s. Whatever the reason, it was a catchy moniker and a bit surprising because Andre was such an easy-going guy. His teammates in Cleveland even dubbed the whirlpool in the locker room the *USS Thunder* whenever Andre soaked in it.

Andre continued his solid play over 10 seasons in Cleveland. He also was a good fielder. Andre, at 6 foot 2, could pound the ball. He is the all-time home-run leader at Municipal Stadium, the giant old park where the Indians used to play. In a game in 1978, Andre became only the sixth Cleveland player since 1903 to hit for the cycle, meaning he had a single, double, triple, and home run in the same game. "When I face Cleveland, I just want to be able to pitch around Thornton. He'll turn my 1–0 win into a 2–1 loss," Jim Palmer, a great pitcher for the Baltimore Orioles, once said.[6] Unfortunately, the Indians were not a great team when Andre played. "We either had teams with good hitters, or good pitchers," he said. "Never enough of both."[7]

The fans and media remember Andre's accomplishments on the field as a clutch player, but also what he did off the field. People thought of him as modest and someone who expressed his thoughts clearly. He endured a great tragedy and many injuries, yet he never quit. He missed the entire 1980 season because of knee surgery. In 1978, he won the Danny Thompson Memorial Award for his Christian spirit. A year later, he was named winner of the Roberto Clemente Award, a high honor to the ballplayer who contributes to his team and to society. Clemente was a Puerto Rican–born baseball player who finished his career with exactly 3,000 hits. He played his entire career with the Pittsburgh Pirates and died at age 38 while helping to coordinate relief efforts for victims of an earthquake in Nicaragua. He is in the Hall of Fame.

The honors continued in 1982. Andre became the first Indian to win the Fred Hutchinson Award, given to the player who overcomes adversity and shows good character and a "fighting spirit." And he was awarded the Comeback Player of the Year. Even though Andre has said there are more important priorities in life than awards, they showed how much the media and the league thought of Andre as a person, as well as a ballplayer. "I believe Thornton is the first player in baseball to receive the Danny Thompson, Roberto Clemente, Fred Hutchinson and Comeback Player of the Year award," said an executive with the Indians, Phil Seghi, on January 14, 1983, which had been declared "Andre Thornton Day."[8]

Andre married a woman named Gail, who sang in a group that recorded gospel music. She even once sang the National Anthem before a game in Cleveland. After he retired in 1987, Andre and his family remained in the Cleveland area. He runs a successful company that deals with warehouse needs for other companies.

Several years after Andre retired, another tragedy struck the Indians. Two players were killed in a boating accident in Florida. Who was called on to speak at the memorial service, to comfort those around him? Andre Thornton.

Andre says:

- Andre's words of wisdom: "I have the wonderful opportunity to speak to many young people like you who are looking for advice and direction. There are three things that I think are very important to your success."
- "The three things are:

  1. Attitude
  2. Behavior
  3. Communication"

- "Let's take a quick look at attitude; our attitude determines how we react to situations, good and bad. Many people fail at a task because of a bad attitude, which puts them at a disadvantage before they even start."
- "Second, let's look at behavior; your attitude directly affects your behavior. If your attitude is bad it usually causes bad behavior, and bad behavior always produces negative results."
- "Thirdly, let's take a look at communication; we have all heard that people remember the first impression the most. We should always strive to make our first impression a good and lasting one."
- "I call these the ABCs of coaching and they are essential to success; our attitude determines our behavior and our behavior is how we communicate. I'm rooting for your success!"

23

MIKE VEECK, BASEBALL EXECUTIVE

Director of Fun

One time, Mike Veeck was in a grocery store with his son, who dared him to do something funny. So dad thought for a second. What could he do for fun? So he poured a jar of cherries down his pants. For Mike Veeck, fun is what life should be about. After all, he is a man who kept a bubble machine on his office deck and once introduced himself by spinning a top on the desk of his new employer.

Mike Veeck is a team owner in the baseball Minor Leagues. Promotions and baseball are in his blood. In minor-league baseball, promotions are fun nights that often include a theme and are sponsored by an advertiser to help attract fans to the ballpark. They are common for most minor-league games and often include a gift for fans, especially children. His grandfather once owned the Chicago Cubs. His mother worked as a publicist for the famous Ice Capades. His father, Bill, was well-known for coming up with creative stunts to get people to come to the ballpark. To understand Mike, you have to know a little about his father.

Bill Veeck was one of the most colorful and creative team owners ever. The year Mike was born, 1951, his dad owned the St. Louis Browns, and the family lived in an apartment at Sportsman's Park. As a toddler, Mike could romp around the "biggest fenced yard in America to play in, except when the Browns were at home."[1] If you ever watched a baseball game at Wrigley Field in Chicago, you have seen the ivy that clings along the outfield wall. That was Bill's idea. He helped put in the

climbing plant with evergreen leaves. When Bill owned the Chicago White Sox, he created the "exploding" scoreboard at Comiskey Park. When a Sox player would hit a home run, lights would flash and fire-works would shoot out. The unique scoreboard is considered one of the most memorable sports moments in the city's history. For a time, he even had players wear short pants as part of their uniforms. Bill had an artifi-cial leg from a war injury, so he had an ashtray built into it so he could smoke!

"I never get tired of people coming up to me and telling me about my old man. I love hearing the stories," Mike once said.[2] When he owned the Cleveland Indians, Bill Veeck also signed Larry Doby, the first African American player in the American League. He was the first person to put names on players' jerseys, and once even staged a night game when day games were more popular so war workers coming off the late shift could see a ballgame. "He loved the fans. Every decision he ever made was for the fans," Mike once said.[3]

Since Bill moved throughout the league, owning different teams, Mike lived in different places. He was born in Tucson, Arizona, and after living in St. Louis, he grew up in Chicago. He learned about the value of ideas when, as one of nine kids, he was involved in family fire drills. One of the kids was always in charge of grabbing a shoebox full of scraps of paper—ideas. That's when Mike realized ideas must be important things.

Years later, Mike told a reporter, "One thing I know is that innovation and ideas are more important than ever. You can find an audience for a great idea."[4]

Besides baseball, Mike had another love: music. He played drums and guitar and was in a band called Chattanooga Glass. He loved singers like Gene Chandler, Sam Cooke, and Bob Dylan. In fact, he once said he would have loved to have played in a New Orleans-style jazz band in the 1940s or 1950s. He might have kept busy humming some of those old tunes during his first job: shoveling manure at a racetrack. Then one day his dad called, inviting him to lunch. It turned into many hours of discussion between father and son. What Bill wanted to ask Mike was simple: would he like to work with him in baseball? Mike soon found himself at the ballpark on the South Side of Chicago, promoting rock concerts at the park and doing other duties. In the six years he worked for his father, Mike never saw Bill in a bad mood. Father and son worked hard, and in 1977 the White Sox—who were not a very good team—managed to set an attendance record, in part because of the Veecks' work at promotions. It looked like life was going well for Mike, until July 12, 1979.

Mike had teamed with a local DJ named Steve Dahl to promote an event called "Disco Demolition." The idea was people would bring a disco record to the ballpark and get in for 98 cents—98 being the position on the dial of the radio station sponsoring the event. The White Sox had a doubleheader that day. Between games, the records were piled on the field and blown up. The problem was, there were more fans than the team expected. Many ran onto the grass. The explosion damaged the field. The White Sox had to forfeit the game, and dozens of fans were arrested. For Mike, it was a promotion that had gone terribly wrong. Like his dad's exploding scoreboard idea, Disco Demolition became known as one of Chicago's most memorable sports moments. Unlike the exploding scoreboard, this went down as a not-so-great idea. Seven months later, Mike left the White Sox.

From that point, no one in baseball would offer him a job. He drifted to Florida and worked an assortment of jobs, but his heart wasn't in them. Years passed, and Bill died. Then one day, Mike received a call from a man who owned teams in the Minor Leagues. He was looking for someone to run a team in Miami. He called Mike and said, "There should be a Veeck in baseball."[5] It had taken about 10 years, but Mike Veeck was back in the game.

The Miami Miracle would be just the first team Mike would own. Later he joined other investors in buying teams in several cities, including St. Paul, Minnesota, and Charleston, South Carolina.

Mike went to work immediately. He didn't want to do anything the ordinary way. In St. Paul, instead of having batboys deliver baseballs to the umpire at the start of the game, Mike had a pig do it. (When Brett Favre played football for the Minnesota Vikings, the pig's name was *Brat* Favre.) And instead of having the umpire dust off the plate at the beginning of the game, Mike had a man dressed as a butler do it—with a vacuum cleaner. He created "Mime-O-Vision" where, after a close play, several mimes would jump atop a dugout and reenact what happened. Mimes are comedic actors who portray a scene or activity using only wordless gestures and body movements. (Fans hated that so much they kept buying hot dogs to throw at the mimes!) That was one of Mike's favorite promotions, along with good ol' fireworks, which are used at many stadiums across the country.

He installed fun-house mirrors in bathrooms. Another time in Charleston, Mike held "Nobody Night," where the team set the *lowest* attendance record—zero fans. Mike and his staff kept the gates locked. When the fifth inning came around, making it an official game, fans were let in the park. That one intrigued the media so much, Mike did 237 interviews! He also held a *Wizard of Oz* night with a Dorothy lookalike contest. He does charitable promotions, like "Books for Bats" night, rewarding kids who read books with two free tickets. For Mike, whose title at one point was "Director of Fun," it's all about getting people to go to the ball games and enjoy themselves.

"Promotion is just trying to expose people to this great game and get them to come back. It's that simple. It doesn't seem like brain surgery to me. . . . Coming to the ballpark ought to be a fun thing, where you're thrilled and excited and have a good time."[6] Having a passion for what you do and a good attitude—because that affects those around you—are some of the most important things to remember, he says.

Mike always is willing to try new things. Once, a blind man who loved baseball teamed up with a sighted friend and wrote 176 letters to ballclubs, asking for announcer jobs. They were knowledgeable about the game and wanted to announce. Only one person was willing to give them a chance—Mike Veeck. Another important part of the Minor Leagues is the cost. Fans pay a lot more to see a Major League game. The stars are on the field, and a ticket costs more. But in the Minor Leagues, most fans don't know if they are seeing the next great superstar or not. "When times are tough people come out to minor-league games," Mike told a reporter once. "When times are better they come out in record numbers."[7]

Mike did get a chance to go back to Major League Baseball, when the Tampa Bay Rays hired him in 1998. But something happened. The one thing Mike had wanted—to work again in the Major Leagues—suddenly wasn't fun. Getting things done wasn't so easy. More people had to sign off on his ideas. He found many were not as open to his promotions as they had been in his days in the Minor Leagues. Something else happened. While Mike was working for the Rays he learned that his young daughter, Rebecca, had a rare disease and was going blind. So he left the Rays and took Rebecca all over the country to see different sights and landmarks. Rebecca could become a baseball executive someday, her father once said. She had a natural feel for it and had been around the game since she was in a stroller. In fact, Mike used to keep her stroller in his office, and when people would walk by Rebecca would jump up and say, "Hi!"[8]

Now, Mike devotes himself to making sure fans have fun at Minor League games. His goals are more important than just coming up with promotions to get people to come to the ballpark. He tries to make people laugh every day and to treat people the way he wants to be treated. He tries to stay upbeat and see the positive side of things, even when things don't look so great. One time he broke his leg, but instead of being down about it, he saw it as an opportunity to spend more time with his family and to read more books, which he loves. "Pursue knowledge from books and people," he once wrote.[9] He also gives about 200 speeches a year and, amazingly, rarely uses notes. In one of those speeches he reminded the audience that the average adult laughs about 30 times a day, but the average child laughs about 300 times a day. His message always remains clear: "Fun is good. It's a basic human need."[10]

Mike once said of his father, "He had fun. But first and foremost he loved this game."[11] The same could be said for Mike.

Mike says:

- Mike's favorite books: "*The Wizard of Oz, The Gnome King, The Scarecrow of Oz*, and *Dorothy in Oz* by L. Frank Baum. People don't realize *The Wizard of Oz* was but one of 17 delightful trips to the imaginative land of Oz. They were immensely readable, entertaining, great art (N. C. Wyeth) and all together they constructed an enchanting land where all was right. It layered the strength of dreams, the courage of convictions and a playful non-preachy style. If one were to get philosophical—life on three or four different levels. It was the first writing that I could see in color—unlike Jack London or J. J. Cooper. Vibrant photographs in my mind—Rube Goldberg machines, the ultimate use of imagination."
- Mike's words of wisdom: "Have fun, be good to mom and help all you can."
- "Be your own person. I was Bill's boy until I was 15."
- "Emulate the great traits of adults but forge your own."

L. Frank Baum (1856–1919) was an author known for The Wizard of Oz, *a book that came out in 1900 about a girl named Dorothy who, as a tornado is descending upon her home in Kansas, suddenly dreams she is in a land of witches (good and bad) and other characters along with her dog, Toto. It was made into a famous movie in 1939 that is still shown on television. Jack London (1876–1916) was a world traveler who became a writer of adventure stories. Rube Goldberg machines are based on the creation of cartoonist Rube Goldberg (1883–1970). They are elaborate, fun "machines" that anyone can create to help a person do one simple task.*

NOTES

I. BRIAN BOITANO, FIGURE SKATING

1. Pat Jordan, "The second time around," *Los Angeles Times*, February 13, 1994.
2. Michelle Kaufman, "Boitano, he's back," *Detroit Free Press*, January 3, 1994.
3. Brian Boitano with Suzanne Harper, *Boitano's Edge* (New York: Simon & Schuster, 1997), 28.
4. Donna Kato, "Brian on Axel's popular hometown skater," *San Jose Mercury News*, July 12, 1996.
5. Boitano, *Boitano's Edge*, 105.
6. Karen Adams, "His dream came true," *The Roanoke Times*, February 9, 1996.

2. BOBBY BOWDEN, FOOTBALL

1. Bob Hersom, "Father Football: The Bowden family is synonymous with success," *Daily Oklahoman*, December 23, 2000.
2. Bobby Bowden with Steve Bowden, *The Bowden Way* (Marietta, GA: Longstreet Press, 2001), 147–48.
3. Hersom, "Father Football."
4. Scott Carter, "Bobby Bowden returns to his roots for the first meeting between FSU and Alabama since 1974," *Tampa Tribune*, September 25, 2007.
5. Bowden, *The Bowden Way*, 178.
6. Bowden, *The Bowden Way*, 31.

7. Bowden, *The Bowden Way*, 31.

8. Bowden, *The Bowden Way*, 228–29.

9. Doug Segrest, "Loaded for Bear: Bear Bryant's Division I-A record for wins will be passed this season—perhaps twice," *Birmingham News*, August 26, 2001.

10. Mark Blaudschun, "Bowden not retiring kind at 70, he loves the job too much to call it quits," *Boston Globe*, January 1, 2000.

11. Brian Landman, "A back yard in Birmingham marks origin of a legend," *St. Petersburg Times*, December 5, 2006.

3. DAVE BURBA, BASEBALL

1. Brad Schmaltz, "Burba among best of former Buckeyes; the Red player ranks among the top Major League pitchers produced by Ohio State," *Columbus Dispatch*, May 18, 1997.

2. Tom Randall, personal interview, August 16, 2011.

3. Marc Katz, "Major League pitchers give back to Kenton Ridge," *Dayton Daily News*, May 2, 1996.

4. Randall, personal interview, August 16, 2011.

5. Brad Bournival, "Ex-Indian gets back into the game," *Akron Beacon Journal*, August 11, 2016.

4. TODD CHRISTENSEN, FOOTBALL

1. John Freeman, "Christensen has a way with words," *San Diego Union-Tribune*, September 14, 1990.

2. Bill Lyon, *When the Clock Runs Out* (Chicago: Triumph Books, 1999), 243.

3. Jim Murray, "This Raider likes to do it his way," *Los Angeles Times*, September 22, 1987.

4. Tom Needham, *Oakland Raiders* (Edina, MN: ABDO Publishing Co., 2010), 35.

5. Jim Murray, "He went from Raiders to Gladiators," *Los Angeles Times*, April 19, 1990.

6. Thomas N. Domer, "Letters from readers," *Milwaukee Journal Sentinel*, November 1, 1988.

7. Sam Farmer, "Ends of an Era: Rookie tight end Dudley in a position to follow greatness with Raiders," *San Jose Mercury News*, May 3, 1996.

5. FRANK DEFORD, SPORTSWRITING

1. Glenn F. Bunting, "Picking nits with Frank Deford: In the hyperbolic world of sports journalism, the Sports Illustrated icon is considered a master storyteller. And most of the time, he gets it right," *Los Angeles Times*, January 11, 2004.

2. Michael Ollove, "Coming home: Sportswriter Frank Deford recalls what it was like growing up in Baltimore," *Baltimore Sun*, May 2, 2001.

3. Ollove, "Coming home."

4. Bunting, "Picking nits with Frank Deford."

5. Brandon Griggs, "Frank Deford knows the score: Author and commentator will share his insights into the sporting life at free library lecture," *Salt Lake Tribune*, August 22, 2004.

6. Ray Routhier, "Sportswriter's game? Not games," *Portland (Maine) Press Herald*, January 27, 2005.

7. Mike Allende, "Deford to paint a broader picture of sports for WWU speech," *Bellingham (Wash.) Herald*, May 4, 2003.

6. TONY DUNGY, FOOTBALL

1. Christopher Price, *The Blueprint* (New York: Thomas Dunne Books, 2007), 227.

2. L. C. Johnson, "Tony Dungy: Low-key style of Bucs coach masks intense competitiveness," *Orlando Sentinel*, January 23, 2000.

3. Leland Stein, "Tony Dungy: One of a kind," *Michigan Chronicle*, January 21–29, 2009.

4. Jarrett Bell, "Opportunity leads Dungy to Hall," *Honolulu Star-Advertiser*, August 1, 2016.

7. MIKE ERUZIONE, HOCKEY

1. Mike Eruzione and Neal R. Boudette, "Cold War," *The Boston Globe*, December 29, 2019, excerpted from *The Making of a Miracle* (Harper Publishers, 2020).

2. Eruzione and Boudette, "Cold War."

3. Eruzione and Boudette, "Cold War."

4. Skip Myslenski, "Eruzione still reliving miracle of Lake Placid," *Chicago Tribune*, January 3, 1988.

5. Rachel Blount and John Millea, "Miracle on Ice, 20th anniversary, frozen in time," *(Minneapolis) Star Tribune*, February 22, 2000.

6. Ted Hutton, "Life after the miracle: Golden young men have grown into businessmen and fathers, still touched by the spirit of that 1980 team," *South Florida Sun-Sentinel*, February 8, 2002.

7. Eruzione and Boudette, "Cold War."

8. GERRY FAUST, FOOTBALL

1. Jerry Crowe, "For him, the Notre Dame job was a Faustian bargain," *Los Angeles Times*, November 24, 2008.

2. Peter Richmond, "Faust: Made in the mold," *Miami Herald*, September 23, 1983.

3. Gary Pomerantz, "Notre Dame's Faust is bid a rude farewell," *Washington Post*, December 1, 1985.

4. Frank Corsoe, "Scouting the Dayton sports scene," *Dayton Daily News*, October 7, 2001.

5. Joe Layden, *Notre Dame Football: A to Z* (Dallas: Taylor Publishing, 1997), 90.

6. Gerry Faust with Steve Love, *The Golden Dream* (Champaign, IL: Sports Publishing, 1997), 244.

7. Faust, *The Golden Dream*, 51.

8. Crowe, "For him, the Notre Dame job was a Faustian bargain."

9. Faust, *The Golden Dream*, 319.

9. TONY GRANATO, HOCKEY

1. Bob Verdi, "Chicago to Calgary: Warm family on ice," *Chicago Tribune*, February 15, 1988.

2. Karen Brandon, "Granato's hockey future uncertain," *Chicago Tribune*, February 24, 1996.

3. Mike Kiley, "Trade could be on Hawks' wish list; Kings' Granato a perfect fit," *Chicago Tribune*, December 23, 1993.

4. Kevin Allen, "U.S. rookies put Rangers in paradise," *USA Today*, January 30, 1989.

5. Ross McKeon, "Granato relishing his 'second' life," *The Patriot Ledger* (Quincy, Mass.), September 18, 1996.

6. Bran Hanley, "Kings' Granato better, but return uncertain," *Chicago Sun-Times*, March 10, 1996.

7. Neil Milbert, "The latest phase of his dream," *Chicago Tribune*, February 17, 2003.

8. Dennis Punzel, "Not on short list, Granato introduced as new coach," *Stevens Point Journal* (Stevens Point, Wis.), March 31, 2006.

9. Tim Tierney, "Bad breaks a pain to Granato, Wisconsin," *Chicago Tribune*, February 10, 1986.

10. TIM GREEN, FOOTBALL

1. Larry Stewart, "Green is Renaissance man of sports," *Los Angeles Times*, September 23, 1994.

2. Rachel Coker, "Athlete, lawyer, broadcaster, author: Tim Green has packed many careers and 10 books into 39 years," *Press & Sun-Bulletin* (Binghamton, N.Y.), January 26, 2003.

3. Jim Alexander, "Falcon Green's career option a novel choice," *Press Enterprise* (Riverside, Calif.), November 13, 1993.

4. J. Edwin Smith, "Literary work," *The Sporting News*, February 8, 1993.

5. Tim Green, *The Dark Side of the Game* (New York: Warner Books, 1996), 2.

6. Green, *The Dark Side of the Game*, 2–3.

7. Green, *The Dark Side of the Game*, 264.

8. Marc Bona, "Talking with Tim Green," *AudioFile magazine*, August–September 2009.

9. "Former NFL star-turned author, Tim Green, visits Fulton schools," *The (Syracuse) Post-Standard*, October 21, 2010.

10. Paul Lomartire, "Tim Green's latest career: Blockbuster novelist," *Cox News Service*, October 15, 1999.

11. Steve Kroft, "Tim Green: Coping with the ALS he thinks was caused by the game he loves," *cbsnews.com*, November 18, 2018, accessed from: https://www.cbsnews.com/news/tim-green-coping-with-the-als-he-thinks-was-caused-nfl-atlanta-falcons-syracuse-football-60-minutes/.

11. JANET GUTHRIE, AUTO RACING

1. Janet Guthrie, *Janet Guthrie: A Life at Full Throttle* (Toronto: Sport Media Publishing Inc., 2005), 277.

2. Guthrie, *Janet Guthrie*, 120.

3. Guthrie, *Janet Guthrie*, 129.

4. Guthrie, *Janet Guthrie*, 356.

5. Mike Malloy, "Auto racing: Indy 500 historian recalls Iowan Janet Guthrie's mettle," *Des Moines Register*, April 22, 2011.

12. LOU HOLTZ, FOOTBALL

1. Regis Behe, "Determination helped Notre Dame's Holtz find his place," *Pittsburgh Tribune-Review*, August 27, 2006.

2. Dana Hunsinger Benbow, "ND president takes issue with Holtz' speech," *Indianapolis Star*, August 28, 2020.

3. Lou Holtz, *Wins, Losses, and Life Lessons* (New York: William Morrow, 2006), 18.

4. Holtz, *Wins, Losses, and Life Lessons*, 26–27.

5. Holtz, *Wins, Losses, and Life Lessons*, 128.

6. Holtz, *Wins, Losses, and Life Lessons*, 187.

7. Sally Jenkins, "Holtz named by Notre Dame; ex-Minnesota coach, at 48, gets the job he has always wanted," *Washington Post*, November 28, 1985.

8. Brian Windhorst, "Sideline Savior Holtz has just one plan—to win—and has done so, school after school," *Akron Beacon Journal*, December 31, 2000.

9. Holtz, *Wins, Losses, and Life Lessons*, 154.

10. David Haugh, "Holtz will carry love of Notre Dame to his grave, *South Bend (Ind.) Tribune*, April 21, 1999.

13. TOM KURVERS, HOCKEY

1. Tom Saterdalen, personal interview via email, March 4, 2012.

2. Saterdalen, personal interview, March 4, 2012.

3. Adam Wodon, "Catching up with . . . Tom Kurvers," *College Hockey News*, December 20, 2000.

4. Ron Fimrite, "A flame that burned too brightly," *Sports Illustrated* via si.com March 18, 1991, retrieved March 4, 2012.

5. Donna Cassata, "Sports News," *Associated Press*, March 24, 1984.

6. Kevin Pates, "Memories, pain still vivid from epic 1984 title game: Rematch: UMD and Bowling Green meet for first time since the Bulldogs lost the four-overtime heartbreaker," *Duluth News-Tribune* (Minn.), January 2, 2004.

7. Wodon, *College Hockey News*, December 20, 2000.

8. Saterdalen, personal interview, March 4, 2012.

9. Jack Falla, "Alors! Look who's coming to dinner," *Sports Illustrated* via si.com, November 19, 1984, retrieved March 4, 2012.

10. Pates, "Memories, pain still vivid from epic 1984 title game."

11. Mark Hermann, "The windup," *Newsday*, September 24, 1995.

12. Karen Crouse, "King happy to get rid of number," *Orange County Register*, September 20, 1995.

13. Michael Russo, "Diagnosed with lung cancer, Wild's Tom Kurvers prepares for his toughest battle," *The Athletic*, February 8, 2019.

14. VERNON LAW, BASEBALL

1. Don Hoak, "Confidence brought us big victory over Yankees," *Pittsburgh Post-Gazette*, October 13, 2010.

2. Walter Meyer, Baseballsavvy.com/w_law.html, November 24, 2009.

3. Joe Guzzardi, baseballpastandpresent.com/2010/06/30/vern-law-recalls-his-18-inning-masterpiece-from-1955, retrieved March 17, 2012.

4. John Moody, *Kiss It-Goodbye: The Mystery, the Mormon, and the Moral of the 1960 Pittsburgh Pirates* (Salt Lake City, Utah: Shadow Mountain, 2010).

5. Richard Deitsch, "Vernon Law, Pirate Ace," si.com, May 22, 2000.

6. Joe Gergen, "Remembering how the Pirates became world champs in 1960," *Los Angeles Times* (via Newsday), August 8, 1990.

7. Mark Cardon, "Celebrity golf classic doesn't lack for names," *Sarasota Herald-Tribune*, February 28, 2008.

8. Moody, *Kiss It-Goodbye*, 261.

9. Moody, *Kiss It-Goodbye*, 348.

10. Moody, *Kiss It-Goodbye*, 356.

11. Moody, *Kiss It-Goodbye*, 359.

12. Charley Feeney, "Vern Law ending Buc pitching career," *Pittsburgh Post-Gazette*, August 30, 1967.

13. Deborah Carl, "Vern Law on Vern Law," Mormonstoday.com/010810/S2VLaw01.shtml, retrieved March 17, 2012.

14. Nathan Morley, "BYU baseball legacy began with grandpa," Newsnet.byu.edu/story.cfm/50105, April 30, 2004, retrieved March 17, 2012.

15. Scott Taylor, "Place in history: Famous HR was key, but Vern Law played a role, too," *Deseret Morning News* (Utah), October 13, 2005.

15. KRISTINE LILLY, SOCCER

1. Wayne Coffey, "Lilly blossomed like no other," *Daily News* (New York), January 23, 2011.

2. George Vecsey, "Veteran Lilly does job," *New York Times*, July 11, 1999.

3. Jim Trecker, Charles Miers, J. Brett Whitesell, *Women's Soccer, the Game and the World Cup* (New York: Universe Publishing, 1999), 37.

4. Daniel P. Jones, "Laudation for Lilly: Hometown honors World Cup heroine," *Hartford Courant*, August 1, 1999.

5. Jeff Jacobs, "Just count her among the best." *Hartford Courant*, July 11, 2007.

6. Frank Dell'Apa, "Oh boy, Lilly was one of the best," *Boston Globe*, May 22, 2011.

7. Associated Press, "Lilly ends playing career," *Hartford Courant*, January 6, 2011.

8. Coffey, "Lilly blossomed like no other."

16. KIM MULKEY, BASKETBALL

1. Bill Campbell, "Tickfaw's pigtailed marvel: Competitive fires drove Mulkey to perfection," *Times-Picayune*, June 22, 1993.

2. Campbell, "Tickfaw's pigtailed marvel."

3. Kim Mulkey with Peter May, *Won't Back Down: Teams, Dreams, and Family* (Philadelphia: Da Capo Press, 2007), 27, 40.

4. Mulkey, *Won't Back Down*, 63.

5. William Kalec, "In a word, Mulkey-Robertson one 'intense' coach," *Times-Picayune*, April 5, 2000.

6. Mulkey, *Won't Back Down*, 114.

7. Wire services. "NCAA women's tournament," *Denver Post*, March 27, 2012.

8. Chuck Carlton, "Mulkey made a run at Stanford standout," *Dallas Morning News*, April 1, 2012.

9. Bruce Brown, "Hall of Famer Mulkey part of state's great sports history," *Daily Advertiser* (Lafayette, Louisiana), July 25, 2006.

17. TY MURRAY, RODEO

1. Carolyn White, "Texan, 21, rewrites rodeo records," *USA Today*, December 7, 1990.

2. Kimberly Kaiser, "Ty Murray to visit Tingley and his 'second hometown,'" *Albuquerque Tribune*, March 27, 1997.

3. Ty Murray with Steve Eubanks, *King of the Cowboys* (New York: Atria Books, 2003), 55-56.

4. Murray, *King of the Cowboys*, 215.

5. Murray, *King of the Cowboys*, 227.

6. Murray, *King of the Cowboys*, 21.

18. VICTOR OLADIPO, BASKETBALL

1. Jim Ayello, "Pacers' Oladipo gets All-Star call," *Indianapolis Star*, January 24, 2018.

2. Dustin Dopirak, "Embracing Oladipo: Junior's infectious personality, unselfish nature make him Hoosier Nation favorite," *Reporter-Times* (Martinsville, Ind.) January 19, 2013.

3. Dopirak, "Embracing Oladipo."

4. Joe Rexrode, "Alone at the top," *Detroit Free Press*, February 20, 2013.

5. Terry Hutchins, *Indianapolis Star*, January 10, 2013.

6. Associated Press, "IU's Oladipo, Zeller drafted in top 4," *Tipton County Tribune* (Tipton, Ind.), June 28, 2013.

7. Phil Richards, "Crean envisions big things for Oladipo, Zeller," *Indianapolis Star*, June 29, 2013.

8. Alysha Tsuji, "Victor Oladipo beautifully sang 'I Believe I Can Fly' for the NBA Talent Challenge," usatoday.com via https://ftw.usatoday.com/2017/02/victor-oladipo-thunder-i-believe-i-can-fly-sing-song-nba-talent-challenge-all-star-weekend-beautiful-video-watch, February 18, 2017.

9. Marc J. Spears, "How a major injury made Victor Oladipo more tech-savvy," theundefeated.com via https://theundefeated.com/features/how-a-major-injury-made-victor-oladipo-more-tech-savvy/, June 28 2019.

10. David Lindquist, "Pacers' Oladipo: 'Give my music a chance,'" *Indianapolis Star*, November 30, 2018.

11. Josh Robbins, "O'Quinn sees playing time drop," *Orlando Sentinel*, March 6, 2015.

12. Brian Schmitz, "Magic rookie guard Oladipo is an action figure at any position," *Orlando Sentinel*, December 30, 2013.

13. Clifton Brown, "Stephenson, Oladipo lead comeback," *Indianapolis Star*, November 19, 2017.

14. Clifton Brown, "Sunshine State trip ends on a high note," *Indianapolis Star*, November 17, 2017.

15. Clifton Brown, "Oladipo surprises with his leadership," *Indianapolis Star*, November 23, 2017.

16. Clifton Brown, "Oladipo's career-high 47 keeps win streak alive," *Indianapolis Star*, December 11, 2017.

17. Dakota Crawford, "Oladipo tops guards in first-team votes," *Indianapolis Star*, May 24, 2018.

18. Indiana Pacers press conference, https://www.youtube.com/watch?v=Gy3wQTVXIFQ, September 27, 2019.

19. Staff, "Hulls, Oladipo enjoyed overseas trip," *Courier-Journal* (Louisville, Ky.), June 12, 2011.

20. Nate Turner, "Oladipo embraces African heritage," *Indianapolis Star*, August 4, 2017.

21. Turner, "Oladipo embraces African heritage."

22. J. Michael, "Hungry for more," *Indianapolis Star*, August 19, 2018.

23. Jim Ayello, "Season ender," *Indianapolis Star*, January 25, 2019.

24. Indiana Pacers press conference, https://www.youtube.com/watch?v=Gy3wQTVXIFQ, Sept. 27, 2019.

25. *The Masked Singer*, youtube.com, https://www.youtube.com/watch?v=aFeKJ7UXeys.

26. Jim Ayello, "Oladipo has no interest in 'sticking to sports,'" *Indianapolis Star*, October 16, 2018.

19. CAT OSTERMAN, SOFTBALL

1. Olin Buchanan, "Driven to dominate: UT's Osterman a star—Phenomenal season by freshman pitcher turns Horns around," *Austin American-Statesman*, May 16, 2002.

2. Andy Gardiner, " 'Cat' Osterman pounces on opportunity," *USA Today*, August 4, 2004.

3. Matt Arado, "Olympic softball star has roots in suburbs," *Chicago Daily Herald*, August 28, 2004.

4. Rana L. Cash, "Perfect pitch: Cat Osterman's unhittable stuff all the buzz at Texas," *Dallas Morning News*, April 16, 2002.

5. Cash, "Perfect pitch."

6. Jill Lieber, "Cat leaves 'em spinning: Texas counting on pitcher for elusive softball title," *USA Today*, May 19, 2006.

7. John Maher, "Osterman sets out on the road," *Cox News Service*, July 9, 2006.

8. Michael Adams, "Leaving at top of her game," *Austin American-Statesman*, August 9, 2015.

9. Mark Wangrin, "Texas' top cat: Freshman Cat Osterman looks to pitch Longhorns into College World Series," *San Antonio Express-News*, May 16, 2002.

20. LYN ST. JAMES, AUTO RACING

1. Lyn St. James, *Ride of Your Life: A Race Car Driver's Journey* (New York: Hyperion, 2002), 59.

2. St. James, *Ride of Your Life*, 239.

3. St. James, *Ride of Your Life*, 88.

4. Earl Bloom, "Not driven by politics: Profile: Lyn St. James is used to being seen as a woman first and a driver second. But she isn't battling for women's rights today at Indy; she's battling for a victory," *Orange County Register*, May 29, 1994.

5. Stephen Reive, "Dreams, drive, talent overcame racing prejudice," *Times Colonist* (Victoria, BC, Canada) via wheelbasemedia.com, April 25, 2014.

6. Personal letter, Lyn St. James to author, August 23, 2011.

7. Michael Vega, "Her story is history: St. James gains Indy respect," *Boston Globe*, May 22, 1992.

8. Stephen Reive, *Chicago Daily Herald* via Wheelhouse Media, October 23, 2010.

21. DICK SCHULTZ, SPORTS EXECUTIVE

1. Linda Kay, "Schultz: 'I'll always be a coach,'" *Chicago Tribune*, July 13, 1987.

2. Ken Denlinger, "Dick Schultz: The great persuader; NCAA chief sees school pride as source of reform," *Washington Post*, December 9, 1990.

3. Associated Press, "Schultz of Virginia to succeed Byers," *New York Times*, June 8, 1987.

4. Denlinger, "Dick Schultz."

5. Mark McDonald, "Heading USOC has similarities to NCAA," *Dallas Morning News*, September 3, 1995.

6. Andrew Logue, "Schultz changed image of the new NCAA: The former Iowa athlete and coach made over the culture of college sports," *Des Moines Register*, August 10, 2003.

7. Mark McDonald, "Former NCAA chief Schultz named new USOC director," *Dallas Morning News*, June 24, 1995.

8. "Schultz bids NCAA emotional farewell," *Tucson Citizen*, January 10, 1994.

22. ANDRE THORNTON, BASEBALL

1. Andre Thornton, *Triumph Born of Tragedy* (Eugene, Ore.: Harvest House Publishers, 1983), 63.

2. Mike Peticca, "Thunder will reign in Indians Hall," *Plain Dealer*, August 9, 2007.

3. Rick Telander, "Thunder, but no gray skies," *Sports Illustrated*, August 2, 1982.

4. Terry Pluto, *The View from Pluto: Collected Sportswriting about Northeast Ohio* (Cleveland: Gray and Co., 2002), 209.

5. *Chicago Tribune* wires, "Kingman, Haas help A's bomb Blue Jays," *Chicago Tribune*, May 7, 1996.

6. Peticca, "Thunder will reign in Indians Hall."

7. Pluto, *The View from Pluto*, 207.

8. Terry Pluto, "The story of Andy's Thornton's faith," *Plain Dealer*, January 15, 1983.

23. MIKE VEECK, BASEBALL EXECUTIVE

1. Paul Dickson, *Bill Veeck: Baseball's Greatest Maverick* (New York: Walker & Company, 2012), 189.

2. Mike Spellman, "Veeck 'thrilled' about Sox," *Chicago Daily Herald*, October 19, 2005.

3. Brian Heyman, "Ringmaster of the minors," *Journal News* (Westchester County, NY), June 27, 2004.

4. Steve Popper, "Baseball down in the count again," *The (Passaic, N.J.) Herald News*, July 15, 2013.

5. William Hageman, "Thinking outside the batter's box," *Chicago Tribune*, May 7, 2002.

6. Dave Cunningham, "It's Christmas at the ballpark: Veeck will fill Tropicana Field with gifts, joy," *Orlando Sentinel*, December 25, 1998.

7. Joe O'Neill, "Sports Page with Mike Veeck," *Youtube.com*, May 30, 2008, retrieved July 31, 2012.

8. Casey Michel, "Mike Veeck championing stadium for St. Paul Saints; team owner ready to move on from Midway," *City Pages* via citypages.com, May 2, 2012, retrieved July 31, 2012.

9. Mike Veeck and Pete Williams, *Fun Is Good* (Emmaus, PA: Rodale Publishing, 2005), 91.

10. Veeck, *Fun Is Good*, xv.

11. Matt Schudel, "The show goes on," *Orlando Sentinel*, August 25, 1991.

BIBLIOGRAPHY

BOOKS

A Century of Sports. Alexandria, VA: Time-Life Books, 2000.

The American Heritage Dictionary of the English Language, New College Edition. Boston: Houghton-Mifflin Co., 1981.

Boitano, Brian, with Suzanne Harper. *Boitano's Edge*. New York: Simon & Schuster, 1997.

Bowden, Bobby with Steve Bowden. *The Bowden Way*. Marietta, GA: Longstreet Press, 2001.

Deford, Frank. *Alex: The Life of a Child*. Nashville: Rutledge Hill Press, 1983.

———. *The Best of Frank Deford: I'm Just Getting Started*. Chicago: Triumph Books, 2000.

Dickson, Paul. *Bill Veeck: Baseball's Greatest Maverick*. New York: Walker & Company, 2012.

Dungy, Tony with Nathan Whitaker. *The Mentor Leader*. Carol Stream, IL: Tyndale House Publishers, 2010.

Faust, Gerry with Steve Love. *The Golden Dream*. Champaign, IL: Sports Publishing, 1997.

Green, Tim. *The Dark Side of the Game*. New York: Warner Books, 1996.

Guthrie, Janet. *Janet Guthrie: A Life at Full Throttle*. Toronto: Sport Media Publishing Inc., 2005.

Holtz, Lou. *Wins, Losses, and Life Lessons*. New York: William Morrow, 2006.

Klinkowitz, Jerry. *Owning a Piece of the Minors*. Carbondale, IL: Southern University Press 1999.

Layden, Joe. *Notre Dame Football: A to Z*. Dallas: Taylor Publishing, 1997.

Lyon, Bill. *When the Clock Runs Out*. Chicago: Triumph Books, 1999.

Moody, John. *Kiss it-Goodbye: The Mystery, the Mormon and the Moral of the 1960 Pittsburgh Pirates*. Salt Lake City: Shadow Mountain, 2010.

Mulkey, Kim with Peter May. *Won't Back Down: Teams, Dreams, and Family*. Philadelphia: Da Capo Press, 2007.

Murray, Ty with Steve Eubanks. *King of the Cowboys*. New York: Atria Books, 2003.

Needham, Tom. *Oakland Raiders*. Edina, MN: ABDO Publishing Co., 2010.

Pluto, Terry. *The View from Pluto: Collected Sportswriting about Northeast Ohio*. Cleveland: Gray & Co., 2002.

Price, Christopher. *The Blueprint*. New York: Thomas Dunne Books, 2007.

Robinson, Ray, ed. *Baseball Stars 1961*. New York: Pyramid Books, 1961.

St. James, Lyn. *Ride of Your Life: A Race Car Driver's Journey*. New York: Hyperion, 2002.

Schneider, Russell. *Tales from the Tribe Dugout*. Champaign, IL: Sports LLC, 2002.

Thornton, Andre. *Triumph Born of Tragedy*. Eugene, OR: Harvest House Publishers, 1983.

US Figure Skating Association. *The Official Book of Figure Skating*. New York: Simon & Schuster, 1998.

Veeck, Mike, and Pete Williams. *Fun Is Good*. Emmaus, PA: Rodale Publishing, 2005.

Women's Soccer, the Game and the World Cup. New York: Universe Publishing, 1999.

NEWSPAPERS

Akron Beacon Journal
Albuquerque Journal
Albuquerque Tribune
Atlanta Journal and Constitution
Austin American-Statesman
Baltimore Sun
Bay City Times (Bay City, Michigan)
Bellingham Herald (Bellingham, Washington)
Birmingham News
Boston Globe
Boston Herald
Buffalo News
Capital Times (Madison, Wisconsin)
Charlotte Observer
Chicago Daily Herald
Chicago Sun-Times
Chicago Tribune
Cincinnati Enquirer
City Pages (Minneapolis)
Columbus Dispatch
Commercial Appeal (Memphis)
Connecticut Post
Courier-Journal (Louisville, Kentucky)
Daily Advertiser (Lafayette, Louisiana)
Daily Journal (Franklin, Indiana)
Daily News of Los Angeles
Daily Oklahoman
Daily Press (Newport News, Virginia)
Daily Texan
Dayton Daily News
Dallas Morning News
Denver Post
Deseret Morning News (Salt Lake City, Utah)
Des Moines Register
Detroit Free Press
Detroit News
Duluth News-Tribune (Duluth, Minnesota)
Eugene Register-Guard (Eugene, Oregon)
Florida Times-Union (Jacksonville, Florida)
Fort Worth Star-Telegram
Hartford Courant
Herald Times (Bloomington, Indiana)
Houston Chronicle
Indianapolis Star
Journal Gazette (Fort Wayne, Indiana)
Journal News (Westchester County, New York)

Lakeland Ledger (Lakeland, Florida)
Las Cruces Sun-News
Longmont News-Journal (Longmont, Texas)
Los Angeles Times
Miami Herald
Milwaukee Journal Sentinel
Muskegon Chronicle (Muskegon, Michigan)
Newsday
New York Daily News
New York Post
New York Times
Oklahoman
Oregonian
Orlando Sentinel
Orange County Register
Palm Beach Post
Patriot Ledger (Quincy, Massachusetts)
Philadelphia Inquirer
Pittsburgh Post-Gazette
Pittsburgh Tribune Review
Plain Dealer (Cleveland)
Portland Press Herald (Portland, Maine)
Post and Courier (Charleston, South Carolina)
Post-Standard (Syracuse, New York)
Poughkeepsie Journal (Poughkeepsie, New York)
Press & Sun Bulletin (Binghamton, New York)
Press Enterprise (Riverside, California)
Providence Journal
Providence Journal-Bulletin
Record Searchlight (Redding, California)
Republic (Columbus, Indiana)
Reporter-Times (Martinsville, Indiana)
Roanoke Times (Roanoke, Virginia)
St. Louis Post-Dispatch
St. Paul Pioneer Press
St. Petersburg Times
Salt Lake Tribune
San Antonio Express-News
San Diego Union-Tribune
San Francisco Chronicle
Santa Fe New Mexican
San Jose Mercury News
Sarasota Herald-Tribune (Sarasota, Florida)
Seattle Times
South Bend Tribune (South Bend, Indiana)
Springfield News-Sun (Springfield, Ohio)
Star-Ledger (Newark, New Jersey)
Star-Tribune (Minneapolis)
Stevens Point Journal (Stevens Point, Wisconsin)
Sun News (Myrtle Beach, South Carolina)
Sun Sentinel (Fort Lauderdale, Florida)
Tallahassee Democrat
Tampa Bay Times
Tampa Tribune
Times (Munster, Indiana)
Times Herald (Port Huron, Michigan)

Times-Picayune (New Orleans)
Times Union (Albany, New York)
Tipton County Tribune (Tipton, Indiana)
Toledo Blade (Toledo, Ohio)
Topeka Capital-Journal
Tucson Citizen
Tulsa World
USA Today
Washington Post
Wilkes-Barre Times Leader (Wilkes-Barre, Pennsylvania)
Wisconsin State Journal (Madison, Wisconsin)
Zanesville Times-Recorder (Zanesville, Ohio)

INTERVIEWS

Tom Randall
Tom Saterdalen

WEBSITES

allprodad.com
almanac.com
aswglobal.com
baseball-almanac.com
baseballpastandpresent.com
baseball-reference.com
baseballsavvy.com
baylorbears.com
catosterman.com
cblafrica.net
clevelandseniors.com
cnnsi.com
espn.com
f1katewalker.com
hockeydb.com
huskers.com
iuhoosiers.com
kristinelilly13.com
mayoclinic.com
mnhockeyhub.com
money.cnn.com
mormonstoday.com
newenglandsoccernews.com
newsnet.byu.edu
noaa.gov
orthoinfo.aaos.org
pittsburghpirates.com
people.com
pro-football-reference.com
randmcnally.com
retrosheet.org

rhodesscholar.org
suathletics.com
theundefeated.com
usatoday.com
ussoccer.com
uvmag.com
yahoo.com
youtube.com

OTHER RESOURCES AND PUBLICATIONS

Agence France Presse
Associated Press
AudioFile magazine
College Hockey News
Cox News Service
Facts on File
Indianapolis Business Journal
NBC News transcripts
Newsmakers April 1988, Gale Group
Rosewater, Amy
St. James, Lyn
Scripps Howard News Service
Sports Illustrated
Sports Page, Joe O'Neill
The Complete Marquis Who's Who Biographies
The Sporting News
United Press International
Wheelhouse Media

ABOUT THE AUTHOR

Marc Bona is a features writer for cleveland.com who previously worked in assorted editing roles for the *Plain Dealer* in Cleveland, the *Post-Tribune* in Gary, Indiana; the *Times Union* in Albany, New York; the *Detroit News, San Antonio Light,* and the *Dallas Morning News.* Winner of numerous Cleveland Press Club writing awards, he is the author of *Hidden History of Cleveland Sports* (2021) and the football-based novel *The Game Changer* (2018). A graduate of the University of Iowa, he lives in Akron with his wife Lynne Sherwin and their rescue pup Addie. He can be reached at mbona30@neo.rr.com.

CPSIA information can be obtained
at www.ICGtesting.com
Printed in the USA
BVHW042242040921
616062BV00004B/4